TAMYRA HORST

The Gift of Friendship

Developing

and enjoying

relationships

that last

Pacific Press® Publishing Association
Nampa, Idaho
Oshawa, Ontario, Canada

Edited by B. Russell Holt

Designed by Michelle C. Petz

Front cover illustration © 1998 by The Stock Illustration Source

Back cover illustration © 1997 by Artville, LLC

Copyright © 1999 by

Pacific Press® Publishing Association

All Rights Reserved

Printed in the U.S.A.

The author is responsible for the accuracy of all quoted material.

Horst Tamyra, 1961-

   The gift of friendship : developing and enjoying relationships that last /
Tamyra Horst.

      p.   cm.

   ISBN 0-8163-1709-7 (paper)

   1. Friendship—Religious aspects—Christianity. I. Title.

BV4647.F7H67 1999

241'.6762—dc21

                                                                98-56159
                                                                CIP

99 00 01 02 03 • 5 4 3 2 1

This book is dedicated to my very best friends,
Joshua, Zachary, and Tim.
Thank you for supporting me,
praying for me, and loving me.
You are the most important people in my life!
I love you.

Contents

CHAPTER 1

The Desire for a Friend

She lived right across the street. She had blond hair and fair skin and blue eyes. I was the opposite, with dark hair, dark eyes, and a sun-tanned complexion. During the school year, she donned her uniform each morning and headed off to a private school. I walked to the corner bus stop for the public school. She was the oldest of six children; I was the oldest of five. We were best friends.

We did everything together, Ann and I. We crushed petals from her mother's rosebushes and put them in bottles of water to make "perfume." We played paper dolls on my front step and the "Brady Bunch" in her backyard—she'd be one parent and three children; I'd be the other parent and the other three children. We'd take turns being "Alice." We commiserated with each other about how terrible brothers were—she had two, I had four. We planned to always be friends. Forever.

But in the middle of sixth grade, my family moved. My

parents wanted to move our family from the suburbs to the country where there would be more for the boys to do (and less trouble for them to get into). I was angry about the move. I didn't want to live in an old farmhouse in the middle of nowhere with animals. I didn't want to leave Ann. She was my best friend. But we moved anyway.

Ann and I tried to stay in touch for a while. We wrote to each other. She spent time during the summer with me. But it was never the same. Our friendship slowly faded away.

But my desire for a friend, a best friend, a "friend-no-matter-what" didn't end. Like Anne in *Anne of Green Gables* by L. M. Montgomery, I could say, *"I've dreamed of meeting her all my life . . . a bosom friend—an intimate friend, you know—a really kindred spirit to whom I can confide my inmost soul."*

It's a need we all share. A need for someone to talk to. Someone to share our joys and tears and hopes and dreams with. Someone who will dream our dreams with us—and even dream bigger dreams for us than we can believe. We long for someone to listen to our struggles and fears; someone who will understand. Someone who won't condemn us when we make a mistake but who will stick by us, love us, and encourage us to go on. Someone who will be there for us when we need help—whether it's a listening ear, an already-prepared meal, a babysitter at the last minute, or just a hug.

Friends make us healthier. They give us an outlet to share our emotions, instead of keeping them all bottled up inside. Friends become a sounding board. Often, without saying a word, they help us to find the answers we're struggling for. They remind us to take care of ourselves. To slow down.

Friends give us a sense of belonging. This world can be a lonely place. We all feel lonely sometimes. Friends are the ones we can call on at our lonely moments and be reminded that someone cares, that we're not all alone.

Friends make us laugh. We can laugh together. Cry together. Hope together. Be silent together.

One woman said, "Friends offer a less emotionally compli-cated relationship than I have with my family members." Friends don't come with all the baggage of sibling rivalry and family problems. Friends are people we choose to be around because we enjoy their company. Because they make us grow and think.

Friends help us to feel special, cared about. They make the world a little brighter.

God knew our need for friends. He created that need. He created us with the need for companionship. He gave us spouses and families. He created the church to be a group of people who would encourage one another and build each other up. He reminded us of the importance of coming to-gether. He knew that friendship could help us grow. The Bible tells us, "Two are better than one . . . for if they fall, one will lift up his companion" (Ecclesiastes 4:9, 10, NKJV).

God gives us the gift of friendship. It is His gift of love to us, a tangible expression of His love and care for us. Friends are a glimpse of what the friendship He offers is like—friendship with Himself—although nothing can compare or even come close to what a relationship with Him really gives each of us.

The gift of friendship comes in all sizes and shapes. Not all friendships are the "best friend" type of friendships. Nor do all friends meet the same needs in our lives.

Some are acquaintance friends—people we know and see often. Most of our friendships may fall into this category. We smile and ask how each other is, rarely sharing more than "Fine." We exchange pictures of the kids and talk about work, but we never really share those things that are deepest on our hearts—our struggles and hopes, our fears and dreams. Such conversa-tions and sharing touch the surface of our lives but never get past it to the heart. To have a friendship that goes past the sur-face to the things that matter deeply to us, we must go beyond acquaintance and grow into a close friendship.

Close friends are those we share our hearts with. We get together often—in person, through the phone, mail, or e-mail. We share our struggles. Our close friends know our dreams and our fears. They know our children and our husbands. They know the things that really matter to us. These are the friendships that give us strength and encouragement on a regular basis.

Sometimes our friendship with another person is based on something we share—perhaps it's working together, being at a similar stage in parenting, or worshiping in the same way. We have friends who are our friends at work, at church, at the playground, or at soccer practice. We share something in common, and sometimes this is where our friendship begins—and ends.

Then there is the "buddy" friendship. These are friends we do things with, but we never really talk about the important things in our lives. Often men's friendships fall into this category. It's usually harder for men to share from their hearts. They tend to have friends to do things with—basketball, canoeing, golfing. Women can have these types of friendships as well—friends who are fun just to do things with. Whether it's shopping, walking together for exercise, or playing tennis, these types of friendships have their place in our lives too.

Another special type of friendship is that of a mentor relationship. In this kind of friendship, one person "mentors" or "trains" the other in some area or role in life. One friend could mentor another in her career or in her role as wife or mom. Someone might mentor a younger Christian in her walk with Jesus. Mentoring is an opportunity to share the wisdom you have gained from experience with someone else through a friendship. It's helping another to grow stronger as a person.

But the closest of all friendships is "best friends." Each of us will go through life with only a handful of "best friends," if that many. Best friends are rare and to be cherished. Best friends are those who have gone a step beyond a close friendship. These are the people we want to call when something exciting or devastating happens in our lives. They are the friends we share the deepest desires of our hearts with. We trust them enough to be ourselves with them—knowing that they will still love us and stick by us no matter what.

Friendships sometimes change. A once-close friend becomes someone we rarely see or talk to. Like my friend, Donna.

Donna was my best friend in high school. She lived down the road and around the corner. We talked about boys and school and parents. We went out for the school track team together. Donna was the maid of honor in my wedding. And I was the matron of honor in hers. After that, our lives started going different directions—literally. I moved one direction; Donna moved another. Today, months can go by without us talking. I don't know what's happening in her life—what she's struggling with, what her dreams are. And Donna doesn't know what's happening in my life either. Yet we used to talk about everything!

But although our friendship has changed, it's still there. All it takes is a phone call. When my father died, Donna was right there—helping with the boys, listening to me, watching me to make sure I was OK. She worried about whether I was remembering to eat. She spent time with the boys, giving them an opportunity to share their feelings—about their grandpop's death and about seeing their mom so sad. And when Donna was making an important decision in her life, she called me to tell me about it. She knew I'd care and that I'd pray. She knew that no matter how long the time or how far the distance, our friendship—though different—was, and still is, there.

The change in friendships can be sad. It's sad to lose the

closeness we once had. But it's part of life. We grow and change every day. Our relationships will too. And sometimes the change can be happy, like when an "acquaintance friend" grows into a "close friend." Maybe even a "best friend."

Friendships are a blessing in our lives. They add the extra that we need to make life interesting and fun. They remind us that someone cares and loves us. And, hopefully, they remind us of Someone else who cares and loves us too. Life without friends would be like a garden without flowers. Can you imagine that? Just the necessary vegetable plants all in neat rows. All green. No vibrant red tulips. No sunny yellow daffodils. No softly fragrant lavender or roses. No pansies with their faces of purple and yellow and blue. I love color—genuine, bright, deep, alive colors. I can't imagine my yard without flowers. I'd give up vegetable plants before I'd give up my flowers. (Actually, I *have* given up vegetable plants because they didn't grow in my shady garden. So *all* of my garden is flowers!)

Not all friendships will be best friends. Or even close friends. And that's OK. We need the variety of different types of friendships. And sometimes we need different friendships at different times in our lives. No one person—except Jesus—can be, or give us, all that we need. Not our spouses. Not our children. Not our best friend. Our lives are richer, and we are stronger when we're touched and taught and loved in a myriad of ways by lots of different people.

When Mary and I talk about raising our sons, I come away feeling like someone understands. We both have two sons, about the same ages. (Though I wish it were Mary's sons who were experiencing adolescence first! I could use the wisdom.)

Lilly and I can talk about our schedules and our frustrations, about wanting to make sure we're doing only the things God wants us to do, about not being sure what to eliminate from our busy lives—and we each understand the other's struggles, because we are each experiencing that too.

Candace is such an inspiration to me of what a woman's life can be when it is totally dedicated to God. I watch her and listen to her and know that I want to be the kind of Christian woman she is when I "grow up."

And there are so many others who touch my life in their own unique way—Tanya, Cecelia, Minda, Janet, Sue . . . The list just goes on and on. Some are closer friends than others. But all are friends. All are gifts from a God who knows just who I need in my life and at just the right time.

That's the kind of God He is. All-knowing. After all, He created us. He knows everything about us. Even things we don't know about ourselves—or at least don't want to admit to yet. He knows our heart's desires and the deepest longings and needs of our soul. He knows just what we need in a friend. And He will send exactly the friend we need, and the one who needs just what we can offer, as well.

It may be just a brief encounter. Like the day I sat discouraged and feeling alone at my desk. My husband, Tim, was recovering from an accident that left him in a lot of pain and somewhat dependent on me. Plus the boys were little and needed a lot of attention. I was giving and giving and giving—and not getting a lot of sleep. "O Lord, encourage me!" I prayed. That's when Tina knocked on my door. I knew Tina only slightly. We attended the same mothers' group. We'd never had a heart-to-heart conversation. We'd never even had lunch together. Even when she knocked on my door, few words were shared.

"I thought you might be able to use these," was all she said before she quickly turned and left, leaving me a little speechless and holding a box. The box was full of household supplies (guess Tina knew it was hard for me to get out to the store). And in one corner of the box was one of my favorite treats. How did she know? She didn't. But God did. He prompted her heart. And in that split second, my heart was touched by love so warm and big it wrapped around me like a blanket, washing away all those feelings of discouragement and loneliness. I knew that I was cared about—by someone I barely knew and by Someone who knew me well.

At times He may send a close friend. Like when He sent Lilly. My three closest friends had all moved away. A fourth friendship lay shattered in much hurt and heartache. My heart longed for another friend, but my brain said No, that it was better just to keep people at a distance. It didn't hurt as much that way. So I reached out to encourage others but kept walls around my own heart. Then one of those I was encouraging began encouraging me. Day by day the walls came down. Little kindnesses, notes, time spent together, conversations. We thought so much alike. And we were at similar places in our parenting and spiritual walk. Before I knew it, I was right in the middle of a close friendship. And my heart was so joyful. (My brain was too.) God knew what I needed. And He knew who best to send. Someone I didn't even know. A new friend. A friendship that grows on.

God knows the desires of your heart too—whether you are yearning for a best friend or praising Him for the friends He's sent. He sees the pain and hurt in our friendships and longs to bring healing and peace. He delights in watching our friends help us grow—and in using us to help grow our friends.

Friendship is God's gift to us, a gift to treasure and enjoy. It is a source of strength and encouragement. And it is a tool He uses to help us grow in our friendship with Him.

If you are enjoying the gifts of friendship He has given you, thank Him. Pray for your friends. And praise Him for your friends. If you are longing for a special friend, ask Him. Let Him know your desire. Then watch for Him to unwrap the gift of a friend in your life.

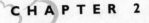

CHAPTER 2

Making Friends

Their friendship began in high school. They had several classes together. At lunch, they would sit together in the cafeteria and talk about their teachers, about boys, and about what they were going to wear the next day. That was forty-three years ago. "She's more like family than a friend," Margaret says about her friend Emma.

Emma laughs and agrees, "We've raised seven kids together—her three and my four. We've shared recipes and problems—and lots of laughter and prayers and tears."

Margaret smiles, "Now we're working on raising grandchildren together. And I'm sure it'll take more laughter and prayers and tears!"

Sandy answered a plea for help in her church's bulletin. "Someone needed a ride to a series of meetings at our church. I didn't think it was a big deal or that it would lead to anything. But the first time I picked Julie up, we just began talking . . ."

Julie interrupts with a laugh, "And we haven't stopped yet!"

Wendy and Stacy have always been friends, for as long as they can remember. They even married men who were already friends. They lived in the same neighborhood when they were both newly married and had babies the same year. They go to craft shows together and watch each other's little ones. They are not only friends but also sisters.

Denise and Judy met at a mothers' group they both attended each week at a local church. "I kind of felt drawn to Denise," Judy says. "When she would share something with the group, I'd think—'Hey, that sounds like me.' So one day I invited her home for lunch. Our friendship just kind of happened after that."

Mary and Mabel are co-workers. They've worked in the same office for years. They talk about their husbands and children. Sometimes they get together for dinner after work or go shopping together. Their friendship has grown slowly and comfortably.

Friendship can begin anytime, anywhere. Often when we least expect it. Sometimes only after we've made the effort to pursue it. But always with time. We have to commit time in order to make friendships begin and grow. Time to get together. To talk.

Friendships also take effort. Effort to keep in touch. To forgive wrongs. To help a hurting friend. To give of ourselves. But our lives will be richer for the sacrifice.

How do we begin friendships? Where do we go to find that best friend who will understand us and love us no matter what?

First, pray. Tell God about your desire for a friend. Then trust His leading. Psalm 37:4 promises, *"Delight yourself also in the Lord, and He shall give you the desires of your heart."* God understands your heart's longing for a friend. He will lead you to the friend who will cause you to grow and feel loved.

Next, risk reaching out. Go places where you will meet people with interests similar to your own. Take a craft class. Join a Bible study. Go to the track and walk. Get involved in your children's school. Most strong friendships exist between people with similar interests—people who have something in common. And most friendships begin at church, work, or school—a place where you normally meet people who share common interests and concerns.

When I was a new mom and staying home full time for the first time, I wondered how I'd ever meet anyone or have time to nurture a friendship. All the ladies at my church worked during the day. When I was invited to a mother's group at a local church, I was hesitant but went. There I found not one but several friends—people who were going through the same struggles I was. They understood about sleepless nights. About never having a minute to yourself— not even in the bathroom. And they understood the struggle to find quiet time for a relationship with God, when every time you had a few minutes of peace to sit down, you fell asleep. We talked. We shared. We got together for lunch. Our kids played together. A couple of us traded baby-sitting so we could each have a "date night" with our husbands.

Chris and Kim met at a Bible study for singles. They both worked long hours during the week but made the commitment of attending the Bible study because they wanted something more in their lives than just working. They get together for dinner and talk about their day. "It was always hard to come home to an empty house after a day at work and not have anyone to talk to," Chris admits. "We meet for dinner, talk, and unwind. Sometimes Kim will come to my house, and I'll cook. Sometimes I go to her house. Sometimes we go out to eat. It's nice having someone who listens.

It makes the evenings alone a little easier."

Mary and Diana met at a soccer game. Each had a son on the team. "We both found ourselves at the park a couple of nights a week. One night we started talking and found that both of us were busy, with no time to ourselves—especially time to exercise—so we began walking together while our sons practiced. I found that I didn't dread soccer practice anymore," Diana smiles. "I actually look forward to it. I'm getting exercise and talking with someone who can relate to parenting, working full time, and trying to keep up with it all."

You may already be involved in places where you could meet new friends—church, work, a club or committee, a sports team. But being at a place where there are people with similar interests isn't enough. You have to reach out. Begin a conversation. Invite someone to get together. Being the first to pursue a friendship can feel awkward. It can be risky. What if the other person isn't interested in getting together? What if she is already busy? Or already has friends?

If you find yourself afraid to be the first to reach out, ask yourself, "What's the worst thing that could happen?" The person could be uninterested in a new friendship. She might say No to an invitation. She might not be friendly. Could you live with that? If you could, then go past your fears and risk reaching out. You may not find a close friendship every time, but you will find some special friendships along the way. One thing is for sure, you'll never make friends sitting by yourself every night. Or by staying in the background at social gatherings. To make friends, you must be friendly. You must be willing to reach out to another person. And who knows? That other person may be sitting there waiting for someone to reach out to her!

Reach out to people you feel drawn to. God may be leading you to someone specific. You may feel drawn to someone you admire, someone who has qualities you would like to have. Janet was someone I admired and respected. She was (and is) one of the most spiritual women I know. No matter what we talked about, Janet took it all to God in prayer. Even when we were talking on the phone about something, she'd say, "Let's pray about this." And we'd pray together over the phone lines. When Janet invited me to work with her in Women's Ministries, I said Yes, more because I wanted the opportunity to spend time with her than because I felt a burden to the ministry. (Though as we worked together, God brought that burden on my heart too.) Janet never sat down and taught me, but I learned so much from her. About prayer. About myself. About God. Janet lives on the other side of the country from me now, but she remains a friend—someone who constantly encourages me and dreams dreams for me that I can't imagine.

You may feel drawn to different people for different aspects of your life. My friend Mary and I talk mostly about our boys and parenting. Our sons are about the same ages. But it doesn't really matter if the struggles we face with them are similar—it's just good to have someone who has similar cares and concerns. Someone who wants to see her sons grow to be godly men too. Someone who worries about the temptations and peer pressures they face. Someone who wants her sons to know how to have a personal relationship with God and not merely live a life of religious habit.

My friendship with Tanya is different than the one I have with Mary. Tanya and I can talk—and sometimes do—every day. About almost anything. I spend more time with Tanya than I do with any of my other friends. Whether it's having lunch or doing crafts or going to garage sales, our friendship is comfortable. I can vent my frustrations about Tim with her, and she knows that I love him and think he's a great guy in spite of how I'm feeling at the moment. She can share with me that she's feeling a little blue and doesn't know why—and I understand. I have those days too.

Sue is my prayer partner. Our friendship has been built on our relationship with Christ. We've shared our struggles and fears and failures. We've also rejoiced with one another over accomplishments, successes, and joys. We've learned to hold one another accountable—in our use of time, in taking care of ourselves, in saying NO when we should. (We both struggle with that!) While we don't often do things together, our friendship is as close as that of sisters; it's one of my greatest sources of strength and encouragement.

Each of my friendships fits into a different place of my life. Some overlap. Others meet a need nothing else does. But each one, though different, is special. Each one is a source of strength and encouragement. God may draw you to different people for different reasons, but each friendship will be rich in blessings.

Sometimes you'll be drawn to people who aren't like you. Someone with whom you may not have a lot in common. My friends Yolanda and Cecelia add a spark in my life that I need. They both know how to relax and laugh, to enjoy life. Cecelia approaches each new project saying "I'm so excited!" Her enthusiasm makes me smile. Yolanda is spontaneous. She instantly brightens up a room with her genuine warmth and laughter. She makes people feel comfortable. Both have taught me to not take myself so seriously, to enjoy and laugh more.

And sometimes God will draw you to someone because of what you can offer that friend. She may not give a lot to the friendship, but God may need you to nurture and encourage her. At first, Paula thought of Amiee's phone calls as interruptions in her day. "Amiee seemed so needy. Every time I heard her voice on the other end of the line, I almost audibly groaned. She was a new Christian. Her husband had left her. The kids were giving her all kinds of problems. One day she thanked me for listening, for caring. She said I was the only person who listened to her and didn't tell her what to do. The only person who prayed with her and for her. I was stunned! I was the only one she had? Then I felt guilt. I had been so self-centered, thinking *What am I getting from this friendship?* instead of wondering what I could be giving. After that I didn't think of her phone calls as interruptions. I thought of them as God's appointments for me. What more important activity could God have for me than caring for one of His children? If He trusted me to love her, then He would give me that love. Amiee has come through a lot. I count her as a friend. There have been times she's been a source of encouragement for me. And it's been neat to see her minister to others who are hurting as she once was."

If God draws you to a needy person, it may be that she needs the kind of love and support He can give her through you.

Another opportunity for friendship is people who are new—to your church, work, school, or neighborhood. They may not know many people and will be open to new friendships. Invite them to lunch. Include them in your plans with others. Offer to show them the best places to shop or your favorite Chinese restaurant. Invite them to social gatherings, even when the event is something they've already received a general invitation to—like a church social. The bulletin may say "Everyone's invited," but a personal invitation will make it more appealing. Having someone to go with or to meet there will help break the ice.

When Amanda moved to the area and started attending church, Carla noticed her. Amanda seemed very quiet and shy. Carla invited her to meet for lunch one day. She was surprised at how talkative Amanda was. Carla started inviting Amanda to help her with different things at church and learned that she had a real gift with the little ones, a gift their church really needed. Amanda became involved in teaching the younger ones and found new friendships with many of the moms. It wasn't long before Amanda felt that she belonged and others wondered what they had done without her.

First, pray and share your need for a friend with God. Then risk reaching out to someone you feel drawn to or someone new. Then what? How do you get past "Hello?"

Often, conversation will naturally flow. You begin talking about the things you have in common. Slowly, you start sharing more of yourself. Don't be afraid to open up. Risk sharing things about yourself. Be willing to be vulnerable. That doesn't mean you need to share every secret and struggle. Just be real. Admit your struggles. Share your joys. When Sue shared her regret at not being a Christian when she was raising her son, Deb immediately identified with her. All the others around the table were young moms or mothers who had raised their children in the church. But Sue and Deb could understand each other's feelings of guilt and regret, their longing to share their newfound faith with their children. It bonded them together in friendship as they began praying together for their children. If Sue hadn't been willing to share her feelings and struggles, she and Deb might never have found a common longing and become the close friends they are today.

Don't try to be what you think others want you to be. Or say what you think they want you to. People don't want someone who is always trying to impress them or please them. Most people want a friend whom they can trust, someone who is honest. That means being honest about who you are too. It might be hard to be real at first. You may wonder, "Will they like me?" Too often our insecurities and fears get in the way of our reaching out to others. We need to come to the place that we can accept ourselves for who we are. Then we will be able to relax and be ourselves around others—without constantly being afraid they won't like us. Remember that God made you who you are. He loves you and needs you to be the person He created you to be, with all the gifts, talents, struggles that He has given you. Insecurities and fears are something I've battled all my life—never feeling good enough, always wondering if others would like me. But as I've grown in my relationship with God and learned to trust Him and His love for me, I've also learned to trust who I am and how people respond to me. How He longs for us to recognize the value He has placed on us and to live in that value!

Dee Brestin in her book, *The Friendships of Women,* suggests that we can start in the middle of a friendship instead of at the beginning. "There's an art," she writes, "to skipping the superficial and beginning a friendship in the middle, and it's tied to asking questions. . . . I've found that with a new acquaintance or an old friend our conversation goes much deeper, faster, if I ask, 'What concerns have been on your heart lately?' or 'What have you been thinking about lately?' rather than 'How are you?' "

Get past the surface by asking questions that go beyond "How are you?" Ask questions such as "What are the greatest challenges you face?" "How have you seen God at work in your life this week?" Talk about things that go beyond the superficial—the weather, work, events—and talk of matters of the heart—concerns, joys, and challenges. If it's hard to come up with questions on your own, the Serendipity Study Bible and the game "LifeStories" are two places to start getting ideas. Both have thought-provoking questions.

Another way of getting past the surface in a friendship—of going past "acquaintance friendship" to a deeper friendship, is to show your friend that you care. That you're thinking of her. I have one friend who is great at showing that she cares, especially when I'm going on a trip. She knows that I get a little nervous about leaving the family and speaking before strangers. So a night or two before I have to leave, Cecelia always shows up with a little something, reminding me of her love—and of God's. Recently I took a trip to Seattle to speak to women's ministries leaders. True to form, Cecelia showed up at church with a little gift for me before I left. It was bath stuff—all rose scented. Cecelia knows me. She knows that roses are a reminder to me of God's love. (She had read *How to Hug a Heart!*) She wanted me to remember that even though I was far from home, God was still with me. And that He loves me, and so does she. Her little acts of kindness have bonded her to my heart.

The Bible tells us how we can show we care. Psalm 116:1, 2: "I love the Lord, because He has heard my voice and my supplications. Because He has inclined his ear to me, therefore I will call upon Him as long as I live." What made the psalmist willing to "call upon Him as long as I live"?

First, God heard. He listened. Actively. He "inclined His ear." Picture God bending down and listening. He wasn't distant. He wasn't half-listening while doing something else. The psalmist had God's full attention. Listening is more than hearing. Real listening involves understanding what the person is really saying. Most of us aren't looking for someone to solve all our problems. We just want someone to listen and understand. We can show that we're really hearing what a person is saying by responding with statements such as, "So what you're saying is . . ." Then repeat what you've just heard her say. Or, "So you feel like . . ." and try to identify the feeling you're hearing. You may not always be right, but you're opening the doors to communication. You're showing that you're listening. That you care.

The second step is to care. God cared about the psalmist.

He bent down and listened. He had compassion. Don't be afraid to show that you care. Don't be afraid to tell a person that you care. Be honest. Don't tell them that you understand how they feel if you don't. When my youngest brother, at the age of eighteen, was killed by a drunk driver, the most meaningful thing anyone said to my mom came from a complete stranger—another mother who had written a letter to my mom when she read about the accident in the paper. She wrote, "As I sit here and look at my two teenage sons and think of you, I have no idea what you're going through! The pain and loss you must be feeling. But I want you to know that I care. My heart goes out to you. And so do my prayers." Cry with those who are suffering. Rejoice with those who are happy. Hold them. Give them a hug. Let them see that you care.

The third step is to respond. God responded to the psalmist. He responds to each of us. He hears. He bends down to listen. He cries with us, rejoices with us, cares for us. Respond with hugs. With notes. Phone calls. Your time. I love the book *The Five Love Languages*. The author, Gary Chapman, explains that there are five things that make people feel loved: physical touch, receiving gifts, words of affirmation, quality time, and acts of service. When you know what your friend's love language is, you can respond in a way that will best help her to feel loved. Sue's love language is acts of service. When she was struggling to get her home office together, our family responded by going to her house and putting her computer desk together. She felt loved and helped. My love language is quality time. Lilly determined what my love language was and has made a point to spend time with me—or at least she offers to; sometimes our schedules are so full it isn't easy! Being able to respond to a person in a way that makes her feel most loved is a great way to show that you really care.

As you choose friends and follow God's leading, remember to choose your closest friends carefully. We become like those we're around. When Tim comes home from work and talks to me, I can often detect words and phrases that I know he's picked up from his friend Ron. I see my boys copying their friends. Or their friends copying them—similar sneakers, haircuts, attitudes. We become like those we spend the most time with, so choose carefully. Choose to spend time with people you wouldn't mind being like.

It's been helpful to me, too, to realize that I don't have to be best friends with everybody. God asks me to be kind and loving to all people, but that doesn't mean they have to be my best friends. Some people are hard to spend a lot of time with. Do you have difficult people in your life too? They don't have to be your best friends. There was one person whom I tried so hard to be friends with. Inviting her here and there. Encouraging her. But she made life difficult. I never knew what kind of mood she was going to be in. Or how she would treat me. It was such a relief to come to understand that while I should continue to be kind and loving, I didn't need to include her in everything. I didn't have to spend all my time with her.

In reality, we will be blessed to have one or two really close friends in our whole lives. These will be friendships that draw us closer to God. That make us more the person He has planned for us to be. And God will lead us, as we give Him our heart's desire and trust Him.

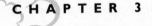

CHAPTER 3

Keeping Friends

Catherine and Margaret have been friends for years. They've been a part of each other's lives since they were little girls, growing up in the same neighborhood, attending the same schools, often double dating, being a part of each other's weddings. They've helped each other through the trials of parenting and now grandparenting. What has kept their friendship strong for so long?

They look at each other and laugh. "I don't know," Catherine shrugs. "I just can't imagine my life without Margaret. I don't know what I would have done without her. She's been a part of my life longer than my husband has!"

"We're fixtures, all right," Margaret jokes. "We've been through so much together and shared so much. I think our hearts are bonded as close as sisters by all we've shared."

"I can't imagine a friendship like that," Diane admits. "But I would love it! I haven't had a friendship last longer than a couple of years. One of us moves, or our lives change. It's just so hard to stay in touch. Life is too busy. But to have someone who is always there for you . . . someone who knows you and loves you . . . someone you can count on. I'd like that. But I don't know that it's possible."

Is it possible for friendships to last in today's busy lifestyles? How do we make our friendships last? Why don't our friendships last? What causes them to end?

Most friendships end for one of three basic reasons:

Distance. At one time, most people were born, grew up, and died in the same community. Today, people are constantly moving because of work, school, or family. It's hard to maintain friendships after a move. The distance between friends often causes friendships to quietly fade away, despite attempts at keeping in touch.

Time. Or more accurately, lack of time. Our lives are so busy. We are involved in so many things—work, family, household chores, church, sports, community, volunteering, running our children here and there. There never seems to be enough time for all that we *need* to do, let alone all that we *want* to do. Time for friends often gets pushed out of our busy schedules. Days, weeks, and months go by without our even realizing that we haven't talked to a friend or gotten together.

Hurts. Sometimes our friends hurt us. We feel betrayed. We hear gossip or a confidence not kept. Sometimes friends let us down or are dishonest with us. The hurt causes a wall, and pretty soon the friendship seems irreparable.

Sometimes our lives change. Marriage, new interests, new jobs, a new church—these, too, can affect our friendships. And sometimes friendships just change. Not all friendships will last forever. God gives us some friends just for a time, and while we may feel a sadness when the friendship ends or fades, God has used them to help us grow, to feel His love, to share His love. And that's OK. We need to accept that some friendships will change and end. But how do we make those few friendships—those that we know are forever—last?

Commitment.

Think about the other lasting relationships in your life. Don't they all require commitment? Marriage begins with a wedding service in which two people pledge to join their lives together forever, through everything life brings, no matter what. Our relationship with Christ begins with a commitment too. It began with Christ laying down His life for us on the cross. That's the ultimate commitment. Our relationship with Him continues when we accept that commitment and give our lives to Him, accepting Him as our Savior. Baptism is the outward indication of that inward commitment. And many Christian parents commit themselves to their children at a dedication service. The dedication service is a time when parents commit their lives to their baby as much as it is a commitment of the infant to God. Even without a dedication service, parenting requires commitment. It requires being there no matter what, through sleepless nights, stomach viruses, broken hearts, bad report cards, and dented cars.

Each of these lasting relationships takes a conscious commitment through good times and bad times. You promise to be there for the other person, even when you really don't feel like it. And there have been times in my life when I haven't felt like maintaining that commitment. Times when the marriage seemed to require more than I had the energy to give. Times when I thought I couldn't possibly live through another sleepless night with a crying baby. Times when leaving would have been the easier thing to do—at the moment, but not in the long run. Through it all, I've learned that it's important to remember that although getting through the present moment may seem impossible, living the rest of your life without that person would be more difficult by far.

A friendship that lasts requires commitment too. A commitment that no matter what, you're going to stay by your friend. A commitment to take the time to do what is best for the friendship. The Bible gives us examples of friends who made such a commitment to their friendship.

Naomi and Ruth. As the women left for Judah, Naomi tried to convince her two daughters-in-law to stay in Moab. Orpha tearfully returned to her parents' home, but Ruth clung to Naomi (see Ruth 1:14-18.) She made a commitment to Naomi, " 'Entreat me not to leave you, or to turn back from following after you; for wherever you go, I will go; And wherever you lodge, I will lodge; your people shall be my people, and your God, my God. Where you die, I will die, and there will I be buried. The Lord do so to me, and more also, if anything but death parts you and me" (verses 16, 17).

David and Jonathan. These two men shared such a close friendship that they were like brothers. 1 Samuel 20:17 tells us that Jonathan loved David "as he loved his own soul." They made a covenant to each other that was to last not only while they were alive but forever (see 1 Samuel 20:14, 15). Their parting words are famous, "May the Lord be between you and me, and between your descendants and my descendants, forever" (1 Samuel 20:42).

Dee Brestin suggests in *The Friendships of Women* that friends today can make this same kind of verbal commitment, pledging to maintain the friendship through thick and thin. But she urges that we not make such a commitment hastily. "If you choose to give someone unfailing love, be prepared to pay a price. There are going to be times when it seems easier to say good-bye—because you've been genuinely hurt, or because the friend is needing so much help, or because it simply takes discipline to keep up a long-distance friendship" (p. 113).

Whether the commitment is spoken verbally or just held in the heart, commitment requires us to pay a price. It requires effort and time and sticking by even when you've been hurt. Commitment is never easy.

How did Naomi respond to Ruth's commitment of love? "When she [Naomi] saw that she [Ruth] was determined to go with her, she stopped speaking to her" (Ruth 1:18). She stopped urging her to go back. They traveled on in silence. Was this a pleasant trip? No words of love. No thank yous. Silence.

Silence can hurt. I've been hurt by silence. Ruth's commitment to Naomi was tested the very moment she made her choice. Yet Ruth kept going. To a foreign land with a different culture and different beliefs. To a people whose attitude toward foreigners was often not positive.

When Naomi and Ruth arrived at Bethlehem, Naomi told the village ladies, "I went out full, and the Lord has brought me home again empty" (1:21). And all the while, Ruth, her daughter-in-law, was by her side! How must Ruth have felt hearing Naomi's words? Naomi even changed her name to *Mara,* meaning "bitter." At one time, Naomi had been a pleasant, caring person. That was the person Ruth had known and loved. But the hurts in Naomi's life had changed her. Now she was bitter and silent. She didn't realize all the potential Ruth's friendship could mean for her. Yet Ruth remained committed to loving her mother-in-law and to staying with her.

David and Jonathan never saw each other again after their pledge of commitment. Jonathan's father, Saul, chased David to kill him. Jonathan, himself, was killed in battle, along with his father and brothers. Although Jonathan had been next in line for the throne, David was the one who became king. Yet, David never forgot his commitment to Jonathan. When he learned that Jonathan had a son who had survived, though crippled, David immediately found him and brought him into his house and provided for his support all his life.

Commitments to friendship will be severely tested. Each of us are human. We're sinners, and we will hurt others. Let them down. Not be there for them every time they need us. Betray confidences. Not understand their feelings or needs. Moving past the hurts will require courage and strength. But lasting friendships are worth the effort.

What does a commitment to friendship require?

One of the greatest commitments is the commitment of our time. Each of us feels that we have so little time to do all the things we *need* to do, let alone the things we *want* to do. Yet time is essential to build and maintain friendships. We need to spend time together—talking, sharing, building a friendship. Without spending time together, we'll never know what is happening in the other person's life. What each is feeling. What needs each has. If too much time goes by without talking and sharing, we may find that a once-close friendship has slipped to the status of an "acquaintance" friend. We have lost the closeness. It's true that we can regain that closeness, but unless we make a commitment to spending time together regularly, we will continue to lose it and have to regain it. That's one reason we can make this kind of commitment with only a few friends—those with whom we long to be friends always.

How can we find time to spend together when we're so busy?

Have a regular time to meet. Sue and I meet every Thursday during her lunch hour. It's only one hour a week, but it keeps us in touch. Often we'll also talk on the phone during the week, but we have that hour each Thursday committed in our schedules regardless. If something comes up that forces us to cancel our Thursday-morning time, we always attempt to reschedule it for Wednesday or Friday. Sue and I normally meet at her office in a conference room. But it could be at a park for a walk. The important thing is that it be some place that is convenient to both of you and that you make the commitment to spend time together regularly. If you wait till you "find" the time to spend together, it will never happen. But even after scheduling the time, you have to be committed to guarding that time and not "bumping it" when something else comes along.

Another way to make time for a friend is to share time together doing something you both have to do anyway. For example, running errands, grocery shopping, grabbing a quick lunch, or working on a project. Several times, Tanya and I have gotten together during the holiday season to work on gifts. Each of us works on our own project, but we do it together—at her house or mine. Our time together usually includes lunch and lots of talking while we work!

Or you can spend time together doing something that you both want to do. Take a class, join a health club, or just walking at the track. That's how Mary and I kept up-to-date with each other. Exercise was important to both of us. So we'd schedule our walking time to be together. It was a lot easier to put in the miles while talking with a friend. (I found I could usually do twice as many miles with a friend along to talk to as I did when I walked by myself!)

Besides *spending* time together with our friends, we also need to make the commitment to *give* time. We need to give our friends the time to do the things they need to do or time to spend with other friends.

Julie and Melanie were inseparable friends. They had babies about the same time. They got together every week to bake bread and make granola. They did things with their children together. But when Melanie's children started off to school, Melanie decided to go back to school herself. She enrolled in the local college. Soon her days were filled with classes, and her evenings were filled with housework, family, and homework. There was no time for Julie.

"It was hard at first," Julie says. "I was still home with little ones, and I missed Melanie so much! I wanted to be supportive of her, but I was jealous too. Jealous of her time. Jealous of her new friends. And probably a little jealous that her life seemed to have such purpose now while I was still changing diapers and chasing toddlers." But Melanie's friendship was important to Julie, so she made the commitment of giving her friend time. Time to go to school. Time to be with her family.

"I knew that one day school would end and she'd get a job. Then maybe life wouldn't be quite as demanding for her, and we could have a little time together again." But Julie did more than just fade quietly into the background. She brought over dinner for Melanie's family during exam week. She took the kids out for an evening once in awhile to give Melanie time to study or to enjoy time alone with her husband. And she prayed faithfully. Melanie remembers that time.

"Julie was always there for me—helping out, never demanding time, never complaining that I didn't have time to be with her. She cheered me on when I made the dean's list, and she made my graduation special. Julie's support, despite my lack of time or support for her, bonded me to her. I knew that she was a true friend. She gave when I wasn't able to give back. I'm sure she struggled with things in her own life during that time. But she never asked or expected anything of me."

Sometimes our friends will need space. But that doesn't mean that we need to fade away in the background. Like Julie, we can still be there for our friends, through prayers, support, and encouragement—but also with the understanding that they won't be able to give us anything in return for a while. Of course, it's important that this period end so that eventually our friend can give in return. Otherwise, the friendship may continue to require more and more without offering any promise of developing further. If so, it may slowly fade away.

Giving our friends time to spend with other friends can seem difficult. As women, we often find our security and self-esteem through our relationships with others. We may feel threatened when our friends are building friendships with others and seem to be growing close to other people, spending more time with them than with us. But in a friendship in which both friends are committed to each other, there can be the security that you will still be friends no matter what. "No matter what" includes other friends. In fact, it is good for each of us to have several friends. No one person can meet all our needs. Having several friends offers us more opportunities for interaction with others, to learn different insights and ideas, and to try new things. It can help us to be less demanding on one friend. But it doesn't mean a particular friendship is less important just because we have other friends who meet different needs and have a special place in our hearts.

I have several friends whom I consider "best friends." And I have to admit that I've been tempted at times to be jealous when my friends had friendship with others. I feared that if they developed other "best friends," they wouldn't have time for me. I needed to remind myself that our friendship would last and that I couldn't always be there for my friends. It was good for them to have other friendships. I've even encouraged friends to get together with others and to pursue other friendship. At times I've offered to baby-sit for one of my friends so that she could have time alone with a new friend. It's not always easy. But it's important for us to be secure enough in our friendship to know that it will always be there.

Lilly and I were still new friends when the time came for her to move and say Goodbye to everyone at our church. Including me. She had been with us only temporarily while her pastor husband led an evangelistic series in our church. On her final Sabbath with us, people surrounded Lilly and her husband to say Goodbye. Tearful hugs and parting words filled the foyer. I knew that I, too, would miss my new friend. In the short weeks we had spent together, we had grown very close. She had quickly become very important to me. Yet I stayed in the background. I gave her room to say Goodbye to everyone else. We had made it a practice not to sit together always during the meetings. Not to spend all our time talking only to each other. We knew that we would get together later. So even on her last day with us, I held back, allowing space for others to share the moments with her. I knew that I would have an opportunity to say Goodbye later and that goodbye, for us, wouldn't be permanent. We'd be in touch. We had already promised to write and to get together.

Give your friends time. Time with you. Time to pursue the things in their lives they need to do. And time to be with other friends.

Another commitment every friendship needs is caring—you caring for your friend and allowing your friend to care for you.

It's often easier to care for a friend than to be cared for. To watch for their needs and attempt to meet them. To listen to them and cry with them and laugh with them. And when they see us caring about them and putting that caring into action, they'll trust us more. It will be easier for them to open up their hearts to us and share honestly.

But we also need to allow our friends to care for us, to do things to meet our needs. Why is this so hard for so many of us? Why is it often difficult to ask for help? Or to accept it when it's offered? Many of us believe that we have to do everything ourselves. We should be able to handle it all. Or we don't want to bother our friends. They already have so much to do. We forget what a blessing it is to us to help another person, and in the process we deny others the opportunity of being blessed by helping us.

I love what Dee Brestin writes in *And Then We Were Women*: "Asking for help, rather than being a sign of weakness, is a sign of strength because it demonstrates humility, the recognition that there are times in my life when I need help to carry an over-burden. And if the need is genuine, rather than straining a friendship, asking for help cements it."

Can you think of a time when a friend was there for you during a crisis? Didn't that experience bond you to her? Didn't it remind you of how much you were cared about? Allowing our friends to help us gives them the opportunity to be blessed through blessing us, and it bonds our friends to us in ways that normal days just don't do.

"I didn't want to ask for help. I felt so needy all the time. But I just wasn't sure what I was going to do. I felt so overwhelmed. I knew that Carol would be willing to help, but I hesitated asking. I didn't want to bother her. She already has plenty of things to do. But finally I called her. I didn't come right out and ask her for help. I just kind of hinted that I needed help by talking about all that was going on in my life and how I wasn't sure how I was going to be able to take care of everything. Even when Carol offered to help, I was reluctant to accept it. But I did; I didn't know what else to do." Joanne smiles, "She was right there. She helped in more ways than I could have dreamed of asking! She saw little needs that I didn't even think about and just plunged in and took care of it. I'll never forget that. Never. She will always be a special friend to me."

God didn't create us to do everything alone. He encouraged us to "bear one another's burdens." That doesn't mean I'm to bear everyone else's burdens as well as my own. We're to lean on each other. And when you're leaning on someone, it draws you closer to them, causing friendships to grow closer and stronger.

Another important commitment we need to make to all our friends—not just those who are closest to us—is the commitment to keep confidences. When I surveyed women about friendships and asked what were the traits they most wanted in a friend, trust was the number one answer. We want to be able to trust our friends. We want to know that when we share something with them, it will never go anywhere else.

My boys and I were talking about keeping confidences the other night. Each of them could think of a friend or two who wasn't very good at keeping confidences. These friends were consistently talking about others behind their backs and telling what others had done or said. My boys knew that if their friends were talking about others, they were probably talking about them too. They didn't trust these friends. One incident in particular had shown the boys how important it is to keep confidences. One of their friends had promised to keep a secret for someone. But in school, when that person wasn't there, she shared the secret with others. It had made her popular for a few moments. But the hurt from that shared secret lasted for days and caused many tears. The one who had shared the secret had done so to gain popularity, to feel like she belonged. But her popularity was short-lived. And now she had the reputation of not being trustworthy.

Sometimes, even when we're grown up, we share confidences because we want to connect with others. We don't mean to betray friends. We don't even think about how it would hurt them if they knew. Like the girl my boys know, we share something because we want people to listen to us, to like us. But we end up doing more harm than good.

It's important that we keep confidences. Always. Even when we care. Because we're concerned, we often share confidences in small-group settings so others can pray for the situation or individuals. But even in these circumstances, it's wrong to not keep confidences. We can ask others to pray for a friend for whom we have concerns, but we don't need to share details that would let our friend down or hurt her. Ask yourself, "What would my friend think if she knew I was saying this?" If you don't want your friend to know you're saying it, then don't say it. This advice may be harder for some than others. Tim is great at not sharing things. (He even forgets to tell me things he is supposed to!) I have a harder time keeping confidences. I love to talk and often talk without thinking. It's something I constantly pray about. I pray that God will help me to be faithful to my friends, especially in what I say.

We can make friendships last by committing to our friends that we will spend time together, by encouraging them to have other friends, and by giving them space and help in pursuing things that are important to them. We need to take care of a friend's needs and allow our friends to meet our needs. That means asking for help when we need it. But through taking care of each other, our friendship will grow stronger and closer. As we do this, we will share with each other from our hearts. We need to remember to keep the confidences of our friends—to refrain from sharing with others what our friends share with us.

One of the greatest commitments to friendship is the commitment to pray. We'll talk in another chapter about how a spiritual side to our friendships will make them the strongest they can possibly be. But as we talk about commitment, we need to touch on prayer. The greatest gift we can give our friends is to faithfully pray for them. For the needs in their lives. For their dreams. For their families. Their jobs. Their children or parents who are far from God. Are you praying for your friend on a regular basis? Specifically praying for their needs and desires?

Praying takes time. I've learned to break my long prayer list into several days. I pray for a portion of it each day using Nancy Van Pelt's prayer notebook. (It's available at Christian bookstores.) This enables me to pray specifically for each of my friends—and others. There is a page in my prayer notebook for each friend (or two or three or more if they're a really close friend!). I write prayer requests in blue ink. When God answers a prayer, I write the answer in pink. When I pray, I just go through and pray through all the requests still unanswered. Many of these prayer requests are things my friends have asked me to pray about. Other requests are ones God has laid on my heart. Often, a regular prayer request is for God to make me the best friend I can be. To help me be sensitive to my friends' needs and feelings.

Besides praying for my friends through my organized prayer list, I pray when God brings them to my mind throughout the day or night. And often I pray with friends on the phone or in person as they share burdens and struggles with me. These times of prayer cement our friendship. As God draws near to both of us, it binds us closer to each other.

Recently a new friend called. I've felt drawn to Tina since I met her. We haven't had time to get together yet, except at a Bible study we both attend. Tina's father had died unexpectedly. Because of previous conversations, and as a result of my own father's death several years ago, I knew some of the feelings she was exeriencing. We talked and cried together. I shared with her from my experience with my dad. She shared her feelings and struggles. Then I asked if I could pray with her. As we prayed, I realized how very much I cared about this new friend. God had given me a love for her that filled my heart as I prayed. As I closed, Tina said, "As you were praying, I realized how much I care about you!" God bound our hearts together as we came to Him in prayer.

God will guide you and your friend as you grow in your friendship. He will show each of us how to be good friends. The best friends. Friends for life.

CHAPTER 4

The Hazards of Friendship, Why Bother?

Friendship is a wonderful gift from God. It can bring us encouragement, strength, and joy. My close friends know me so well. They can sense when I'm going through a rough time and are there for me with words and deeds. They know what to do to make me feel that they care for me.

Recently, Tim and I left church between vespers and a meeting we were supposed to attend. During the meeting, a friend came looking for me because she wanted my input in the discussion but couldn't find us. (We hadn't told anyone we were leaving. Even I didn't know we were leaving until we got upstairs and Tim headed for the car instead of the meeting.) My friend became worried. Sue, my prayer partner who knows me so well, said, "Tim probably took her home. Tami had a long day, and he probably wanted her to go home and rest." And she was right! (She was glad to know she had guessed right—that she knows us so well.) She knows how

Tim protects me. She knows how we both think.

When your friends know you that well, they can tell when you're struggling or discouraged. They know what you need. I treasure my friends. They are a source of strength and encouragement for me.

But friendship isn't without it's hazards. There are times when friends let us down. Betray us. Hurt us. Our friends are people, and people fail us—often without meaning to. But even unintentional hurts hurt.

While I was working on the material for this book, I surveyed over one hundred women, asking them questions about their friendships. Only four said that they had never been hurt by a friend. That means that at least 96% of the ladies surveyed had been hurt by their friends. Some wrote that they had been hurt many times. One woman wrote that she had been deeply hurt and wasn't sure that she had ever gotten over it. Another wrote that she knew the hurt wasn't intentional, but it still hurt.

One of the most common sources of hurt in a friendship is a betrayed confidence. A friend shares something with another person that should have remained a secret. As we grow close to our friends, they'll come to know a lot about us. Our problems. Our fears. Our faults. Friendships make us really vulnerable. One of the qualities women want most in a friend is someone they can trust. Someone who won't betray their confidences.

As women, we love to talk. Sometimes we share things without even thinking. Before talking about another person, ask yourself how you would feel if that person heard what you said. If you wouldn't want her to know you had told someone, then don't say it. Sometimes we listen to things we shouldn't. One way to end gossip is to not listen to it. Say, "I really don't think I need to know this," and walk away. Pray and ask God to help you in both these areas—talking and listening. I have to ask God to help me think before I speak. Too often, I talk without thinking—and I regret it later on.

Because we want so much to belong and feel included, we may share things we know we shouldn't (or would know we shouldn't if we just stopped to think for a moment). Sharing things about others, knowing something that no one else knows, can make us feel important. People will listen to us. We're included. But feeling good doesn't always last.

Katie never meant to cause the hurt and problems she did. She had always wanted to be included in a certain circle of friends at her office. But they never seemed to have time for her. They'd sit together for lunch and talk and laugh. Katie wanted to be a part of that, but they didn't make it easy. They didn't talk to her. And when she attempted to sit with them, they never had room or were just leaving. The day Cheryl was missing, that changed. Katie had seen Cheryl the night before at the mall with a new boyfriend. As she casually mentioned this in passing to Cheryl's friends, it sparked their interest. Katie was the center of attention all day. They invited her to sit with them at lunch. They pumped her for information about Cheryl and her new friend. The next day, when Cheryl returned to work, the office was buzzing with gossip about her and her rendezvous at the mall. And, as is often the case with gossip, the story had been blown far out of proportion. Cheryl was hurt. It took time before things settled down and her friendship with those in the office was restored.

And Katie? After that day, things went back to normal for her. The other women at work didn't have the time of day for her. They had been her friend only long enough to get the information she had. Then they didn't need her anymore.

Sharing what you know may make you part of the group for a little while, but it won't make you friends in the long run. You may get a reputation for being a person who can't be trusted. Each of us knows someone we wouldn't tell something to unless we didn't care if everyone else found out. We don't become close friends with people we can't trust. Trust is one of the most important qualities many of us look for in a friend. To be a good friend, or even a respected acquaintance, we need to be trustworthy.

Sometimes we engage in "holy" gossip—sharing things with a friend or in a small group out of concern or worry. "Anne is my best friend; I tell her everything. So when John and I were having problems in our marriage, I shared the situation with Anne. I never thought it would go any farther," Cindi recalls. "Then I heard that Anne had asked for her small group to pray for our marriage. Now a whole group of people knew! That made things a little difficult. John was not thrilled that everyone knew we were having problems. I know that Anne was concerned and thought she was helping by asking others to pray, but I wish she hadn't." We don't have to share details about our friends when we ask for prayer. God knows the details. If we're concerned about a friend and want others to pray, we can just ask for prayer for "a friend who is going through a rough time." No one needs to know the details.

Another hurtful response, when we have shared the deep things of our hearts with a friend, is silence. We've poured out the anguish of our heart, and they just sit there. Silent. We want them to say something. To show that they heard. To indicate that they understand or at least that they care. But they say nothing.

I have a friend who often responds with silence. And I have to admit, she is not someone I feel like going to when I need a friend to listen. I want someone who will respond to me. A friend doesn't have to have all the right words. She doesn't have to be able to solve my problems. But I need her to show that she is listening.

Last night I left a meeting angry and upset. Later, I poured out my frustrations to a friend. He was silent. Didn't say a word. When I finished, he went back to what he was doing. I felt as though my words were an interruption to him and that he didn't really care, that he just wanted to get back to what he was doing.

Later Sue called. I didn't immediately share my frustrations with her. But in our conversation, she sensed my anger and drew it out. She listened. "I can understand how you feel," she responded. "You feel as though you were being attacked." She neither judged me nor offered solutions. She just showed by her words and her response to my feelings that she was listening to what I said. By the end of our conversation, I was feeling better. I felt cared about.

I know my other friend cares about me (he's my husband!). But he doesn't always know how to respond or what to say. His silence doesn't mean that he doesn't care. Silence may mean that the person is just thinking, taking in all we've said. Or the person could be distracted or truly not be listening. It may not be a good time for him or her. But we don't know why the person is silent, and it hurts.

At times, our friends misunderstand us. They don't understand our motives. They misread our actions. Or they don't act as though they care. They may not have time to listen to us or to spend with us. They spend our time together talking about *their* lives and problems and successes but don't give us a chance to talk. In a true friendship, each person should have the opportunity to share and talk. There may be times when one friend needs to talk more. There may be times when one friend is needier than another, but those times aren't permanent. Friends care about each other and want to know what's happening in each other's lives. Although friends may let us down or betray our confidence or misunderstand us or need more from us for a time than they can give in return, these are not the everyday, common practices. Most days, friends don't let us down. They care about us. Listen to us. Understand and empathize.

That is one reason women, when they need to talk, go to a female friend more often than to their husbands. In one survey, 86 percent of the women questioned said they go to a girl-friend when they need to talk. Women are more natural listeners than men. We listen not only with our ears but with our bodies. Leaning forward. Encouraging the other person to continue by asking questions, nodding, saying things to show that we're listening.

If we have friends, it's inevitable that we will end up being hurt at some point. It may not be a big hurt. We may suffer only minor slights, and we will be able to get over most hurts easily. But not always. Whether major or minor in nature, conflict and hurt will happen. In the next chapter, we'll talk about what to do to bring healing and reconciliation to hurting friendships.

There are other hazards to friendship. One of these is dependency. Relationships are important to women. We enjoy talking and sharing, connecting heart to heart. Because of this, we may become too dependent on friends. We may turn to them for all our needs, until we need them too much. It's important to share things with friends. God tells us to bear one another's burdens. But it becomes a hazard to your well-being when you consistently take your problems to your friend first, expecting her to help you find the answer. God wants us to bring our problems to Him and to look to Him for answers. Good friends will point us to Him.

God wants us to share our struggles and problems with friends. I believe that's one reason why He gave us the gift of friendship. He wants us to have someone to talk to, someone who will listen and care, who will love us with a love like His own. But He is also a jealous God; He's jealous for us. He longs for us to share our struggles and problems with Him and to look to Him for answers. He wants to grow us and heal us and guide us to the solution. It's possible—even without realizing it—to lean too much on our friends, expecting them to listen to our problems and provide solutions.

Ask yourself, "When I have a problem, what do I normally want to do in response? Do I take it to God in prayer? Or do I call a friend? Do I ask God for an answer? Do I search the Scriptures? Pray? Wait?"

Going to a friend is part of the answer, but it is not the complete answer. Ask yourself, "Do I lean on my friend too much? Do I share everything with friends, wanting them to tell me what to do? Wanting them to comfort me and help me to find peace?"

If you're turning to a friend instead of to God, then you're on shaky ground. Remember that your friend is a person, a faulty human being. She can't be there for you all the time. She doesn't know all the answers. Even though she loves you and wants to help, she can do only so much. God alone will never fail you. He alone will never let you down, betray you, or hurt you. He alone brings completion—not friends, not family, not even your spouse.

It's easy to expect too much from our friends, expecting them to always be there. It may start out innocently. You enjoy your friend's company, so you do things together. That's a good thing. It's important for friends to spend time together. To enjoy doing things together. But it's a warning sign when you always *need* that friend in order to do things. When you find it impossible to go out and do something unless your friend is with you. It's not good to become so dependent on one person. What happens if she moves or something happens to her? What happens if your friendship ends? We need to have more than one friend to do things with and not spend all our time with only one friend. We need to be involved with a variety of different people; not everyone can be a close friend. And that's OK. That's one reason why it's important to have a wider circle of friends for different times and different interests in our lives. It helps to keep our friendships healthy.

We also need to be able to spend time alone, enjoying our own company. Try spending a day by yourself sometime, doing things you enjoy, eating lunch out. You may not be able to spend a whole day by yourself; it may be only an hour or two. But make the effort to enjoy your own company.

I'm a people person. It runs in my family. My dad didn't like being alone either. He worked four days a week; Mom worked five. That left Dad home alone on Fridays. He didn't like that very much. Mom said that most all their phone calls were made on Fridays—by my dad, looking for someone to talk to or to do something with.

With both boys in school during the day and Tim at work, I do spend a lot of time alone. I try to get together with friends or at least touch base with them via the phone or e-mail, but it's been a growing experience to go out and do things by myself. I've realized that I really don't like shopping. I always thought I loved going to the mall. But I found that I like going to the mall only with friends. It's not the shopping I enjoy but the talking and being with people. So shopping is not something I do by myself. But I've learned to go out to eat by myself. Sometimes I enjoy that immensely. Away from home and the phone and computer, I have found time to read or just relax quietly. I enjoy going to the market by myself too. The smells and sights.

Psalm 62:5-8 says, "My soul, wait silently for God alone, for my expectation is from Him. He only is my rock and my salvation; He is my defense; I shall not be moved. In God is my salvation and my glory; the rock of my strength, and my refuge, is in God. Trust in Him at all times, you people; pour out your heart before Him; God is a refuge for us." God longs for you to pour out your heart to Him, to wait for Him alone to take care of you. He gives us friends to love us and point us to Him. But He alone is our refuge.

As you read this, you may not see yourself overly dependent on a friend, but you may realize that there is someone who is depending too much on you. What can you do?

Make sure that you are the kind of friend who points her friends to God. When someone confides in you that she is having a problem, ask her, "Have you talked to God about this yet? What is He leading you to do?" If she hasn't yet gone to God about this problem, pray with her right then. It can be just a short, simple prayer, but take the situation and your friend to Jesus.

Share verses from the Bible with your friend when appropriate. At such times, books of Scripture promises are great. They can help you find a promise suitable for many different situations. Claim that promise for your friend in prayer. Let her hear you claim that promise aloud. Not only will this bring her strength and encouragement, but it will help her to learn to look to God's Word for herself, claim it's promises, and pray about her situation.

It's also important to put boundaries on our time when avoiding someone who has become overly dependent on our friendship. Never let a friend demand more time than you feel comfortable giving. There will be times, of course, when someone needs more time and attention than at other times. But the demand for excessive time should never be constant. Let such a person know when you're not available. Give her times when you *will* be able to talk to her, listen to her, or spend time with her.

Cheri really cared about Amber, but she felt Amber was demanding too much time. "Amber called every day," Cheri recalls. "Sometimes several times a day. She constantly wanted to go out. If she found out I was doing something, she wanted to go along. At first, I let it happen. But then I began feeling smothered, and I dreaded her calls. Finally I decided it was up to me to do something about it. Either I could limit my time with Amber or I was going to end up not wanting to spend any time with her at all. I cared too much about her to see our friendship end. So when she called, I'd tell her, 'Amber, this isn't a good time for me to talk right now. Why don't I call you?' Then I'd call at another time that would work for me."

At first, Amber was afraid that Cheri didn't want to be her friend anymore. But as she saw that Cheri was still committed to spending time with her and listening to her, she was able to relax and respect Cheri's time.

Another hazard with friendships is the fear of letting others into our circle. We may become too protective of our present friendships and feel threatened when our friends start growing close to other people. We're afraid of losing the closeness that we have. We all have a basic need to belong. We all need to feel that we're part of someone else's life. We want to feel needed, to feel as if we matter in the life of another person. When our friends begin a friendship with another person, we may fear that we'll lose that friend or that we won't be as important to her. This may cause us to react unkindly to the new person. And we may not want to admit why—even to ourselves.

"When Rachel started spending time with Alicia, I couldn't believe my reaction," Nancy says. She and Rachel had been friends for several years when Alicia moved into the area and started attending their church. "Rachel and Alicia *did* have a lot in common," Nancy concedes, "and Alicia didn't know anyone. One of the things I love about Rachel is her ability to reach out to others and include them. But I'm ashamed to admit that I didn't like it when she began reaching out to Alicia. She'd call her on the phone and invite her to get together. When I was around Alicia, I found that I wasn't very friendly. I saw her as a threat to my friendship with Rachel. Once, when Rachel and I had plans to go to a craft show, Rachel wanted to invite Alicia. I was so angry I didn't enjoy my time very much. I was distant and grumpy all day. When I told my husband how I was feeling, he said that I was being childish. Maybe I was, but it was such a struggle. Finally I had to go to Rachel and tell her how I felt. She was so understanding! She promised that she would always be my friend. And she asked me to give Alicia a chance. I did. And now Alicia is one of my close friends too. The three of us have a blast together!"

Nancy found that allowing Alicia into the circle strengthened her friendship with Rachel rather than harmed it. She and Rachel still made time for each other, but now they each had a new friend too. And when Rachel's son was involved in an accident, having both Nancy and Alicia to lean on gave her more strength. Plus with two people helping out, neither Nancy nor Alicia ever felt overburdened. They were able to take turns helping at Rachel's home, being with her at the hospital, and running errands.

If your friend is spending more time with someone new, it may be difficult for you to accept. And it's true that new friendships take time in the beginning to establish and grow. Talk to God about your feelings. Ask Him for peace. You may need to let your friend know what you're feeling, as Nancy did. "When I told Rachel that I was jealous of her time with Alicia and that I felt that maybe she would come to enjoy being with Alicia more than with me, she assured me that we would always be friends, that we had shared so much together, and that these things had bonded us in a way which could never be taken from us. It felt good to be honest and to talk about my feelings. Talking it through helped Rachel understand the way I had been acting, and it helped me work through a lot of what I was feeling."

Good friends will want what is best for those they care about. They will want to see them grow and be the women God wants them to be, reaching their full potential in Him. When you're holding onto something too tightly, it doesn't have room to grow and bloom. Sometimes we need to let go of our friends so they can become all that God intended them to be. Many times He uses people, friendships, and relationships to cause us to grow. We need to give our friends the freedom to spend time with others and to learn from these friendships too.

Our lives are so busy today. There are so many commitments—jobs, home, family, church—that it's hard to find time to do everything we *need* to do, let alone all the things we *want* to do. It's amazing how fast time can get eaten up! On any given morning, the average woman may get up, toss in some laundry, get ready for work, and get her children ready for school. After working all day, she may have errands that need to be done, more laundry to do, household chores, and dinner to prepare. After dinner, she needs to oversee homework and get everyone ready for bed. After all this, there is little or no time left for family—or herself.

In such a schedule, where do we find time for friends? Where do we find time to get together even once in a while, let alone enough time to build strong friendships and really get to know another person? And why even risk the hazards of friendship? Why bother making time in our already overloaded schedules and risk hurt and rejection? Is friendship worth it?

I believe that it is. I believe God intended us to have friends. He created us with a need for companionship. He put us in families and in communities, and He has challenged us to not forsake the assembling of ourselves together. He gave us a longing to connect with others. To feel needed. To love and be loved.

Why risk the hazards of making friends? If you don't risk the hazards, you can never know the joys. True, our friends may let us down; they may hurt us or offend us. They may not always be there when we need them or need us when we have nothing to give. But friends will also love us, care for us, and encourage us.

Friendship brings us someone to talk to when we're lonely or sad. Friends are there when we're happy and just have to tell someone about it! Friendship gives us someone to do things with—and the special memories that result from those times together. In friendship we find another person who knows all about us—our struggles, our faults, our fears, our dreams—and who loves us. Friends help us carry our burdens and pursue our dreams.

Most of the time—in fact, almost always, our friend will be someone we can trust. Someone we can laugh with, cry with, and grow with. Friendship is worth the occasional hurt. It's like a jab from a thorn while admiring a rose. Roses are so beautiful, and they have such a sweet smell. Yes, they have thorns. And occasionally we get pricked. But their beauty and aroma and the joy they give us is worth it.

How do we find the time?

We will never find the time. Our schedules are too full. We have *to make* the time. Find a place in your calendar to schedule time for friends on a regular basis. Patty and Tina meet every Tuesday evening after dinner. Their husbands watch the kids. Marcy and Virginia get together at the track before work once or twice a week. They exercise while talking. Peggy and Bunny took a class together at the local community college. It was a shared interest and a way of spending time together while they did something they both wanted to do. Lisa and several of her friends from high school don't live in the same area anymore. Once a year they pick a place to meet, and they all fly in for the weekend and spend that time catching up.

After we've made the time to get together, how can we spend that time doing things that will deepen our friendship? I asked the ladies I surveyed what memorable things they had done with their friends.

Many of them said that it wasn't a certain specific time that was memorable but the continuing process of getting together and sharing things with each other—simple things such as baking bread or cookies, shopping for bargains, or shopping at "outrageous stores" and trying on things they couldn't afford, attending women's retreats, acting silly and laughing, playing jokes on each other, staying up and talking all night, double dating (you can double date even if you're married as long as it's your husband you're dating! Try recreating a date from your past, something all of you did before marriage.) It wasn't what they did that made time together memorable but the fact that they were together talking and sharing.

Others did have special memories of a particular time with a close friend. One woman had an interview in San Francisco. Her friend, who lived in the area, met her afterward and brought her flowers; they spent all afternoon talking.

Several of the ladies I surveyed told me that they go on vacation with friends. Tim and I have done this, and it's allowed us to really get to know our friends (and them to know us) in a relaxed, fun setting. We've camped with friends for a weekend and shared a beach house several times with a family we love. Even when things go badly on such a joint vacation, it bonds you together—and gives you something to talk about later.

I remember special times with each of my friends. Penny, who went with me for support when I was speaking at a nearby church. Mary, who met me at the park to walk. Sue, who traveled with me five hours to a church—and back—talking with me all the way. We stopped for pizza about an hour from home and ran into our pastor and his wife. I remember playing games till we got silly with Steve and Ann at Sue's house. Working on crafts with Tanya. Spending a rainy weekend at the shore with Donna, Patty, and Teresa. Talking in the dark all night with Lilly at a women's retreat. Exploring San Francisco and the surrounding area with Janet while we talked and shared things from our lives with each other.

Friendship may be hazardous, but a life without friends is even more hazardous. We need to risk the possible hurts without fear. With prayer and unconditional, committed love, friendship is definitely worth the bother.

CHAPTER 5

When Friendships Hurt

We had been friends for a long time. We had shared holidays, joys, sorrows, and snowy winter days. More like family than family itself sometimes seemed, our friendship was important to me. I would never have intentionally done anything to hurt her. But she was hurt—devastated. She wouldn't speak to me. Avoided me whenever possible. Wouldn't even look at me when we passed at church. And wouldn't talk about the problem.

I didn't know what the problem was. I prayed. I asked God to show me what I had done or to show me why my friend was hurting so badly. How could I help?

I tried. I tried to remain kind and faithful in my friendship—sending a note, leaving a small gift or basket of cookies. But my kindnesses just seemed to irritate her more. I didn't know what to do. I had cried. I had prayed. I had tried talking to her. She said there was no problem, but I knew better. Things weren't the same.

Have you ever suffered the pain and anguish of a splintered friendship? Maybe, like my friend, you've been on the receiving end of the hurt. You can't believe your friend would do this to you. You feel betrayed. You're not sure if the friendship can survive or even if you want it to. You don't want to risk being hurt again. You're not sure if you can trust your friend again.

Maybe you've been on my side of the hurt. That side hurts too. You've unintentionally hurt a friend. Maybe you have even *intentionally* hurt a friend but now regret it. And no matter what you do, the damage now seems irreparable. I wanted so much for my friendship to be healed, for things to be as they had been. I loved my friend and missed her. I missed her phone calls and getting together. I missed her laughter. Many days and nights I grieved the loss and searched for an answer to why this was happening and what could be done to repair it? Would we ever be friends again?

Where do we go when a friendship is hurting? How do we begin the process of healing?

Remind yourself of how much your friendship has meant to you. Remember the good times you've had together; let your mind dwell on the good memories. As you remember the fun times you've shared, you may find yourself smiling again, feeling the love and care you felt for your friend before the hurt. That's one good thing about our memories—not only do they remind us what has happened, but they remind us of the feelings too. Relive in your memory the special times you and your friend shared.

Make a list of all the good things you appreciate about your friend. The things she does that make you smile. The way her friendship has given you strength and encouragement. The character traits in her that you admire and are drawn to. What is it about her that has made your friendship strong?

Why do you enjoy her friendship?

As you make a list of all the things you appreciate about your friend and her friendship, it will remind you of how valuable she is to you. This should help you determine if this is a friendship worth saving.

What if—as you try to remember the good times you've shared and to list the things you appreciate about your friend—you can't think of any?

Ask God to remind you of the good points of your friendship. If, after praying and searching, you still come up short, then maybe this wasn't really a friendship to begin with. Maybe it's not worth the effort of trying to repair the damage. Remember that not every relationship is going to be a close friendship. Sometimes, no matter how much we want to be friends with someone, it may not be possible. Sometimes it's healthier just to walk away.

However, if, after thinking about your friend and how much you value her, you know you want to do whatever it takes to resolve the conflict—what do you do? How do you repair a splintered friendship?

First, remember that your friend probably didn't mean to hurt you. Most of the time, when a friend hurts us, lets us down, or betrays us, it's unintentional. Most of the time, our friends want to be good friends. Sometimes our sinful human nature steps in, and we do something stupid.

Talk to your friend about how you feel or about the conflict between the two of you. Sometimes we think that by ignoring the situation, we're avoiding hurting our friend. But this often ends up causing more pain. Kaitlyn hadn't intended to hurt her friend Marie. "I didn't want to tell Marie that I thought she was handling a situation wrong. I was worried about her, but instead of going to her, I told another friend what I thought. I assumed it would stay confidential; I thought the other friend could pray with me about it. Somehow Kaitlyn found out what I had said and that I had shared my feelings with someone else instead of just coming to her. I can understand her hurt. I would be hurt, too, if I were her. I had thought it would hurt her if I told her what I thought, but it hurt her more that I shared it with someone else."

Too often, we try to avoid conflict at all costs. And that includes talking to friends about problems or anger. Many times, we tell someone else instead. Unfortunately, things have a way of getting around, and our friends end up hearing secondhand what we should have told them ourselves.

If you don't want your friend to find out something you said, don't say it to anyone except God. Better yet, tell God and then talk to your friend about it. Relationships are stronger as we learn to work through conflicts and disagreements, even though it may be unpleasant for a time. Burying feelings and unresolved conflicts isn't healthy. At some point, they will surface again—usually during another conflict—causing an even bigger problem than if each situation were dealt with as it happened.

Remember that anger and conflict don't mean that the relationship is over. Anger and conflict are just another hurdle to get over. Working through them can make your friendship stronger; burying them can cause more problems in the future. It's natural that two people will disagree and get upset with each other at times. We're all different, and often we're attracted to people with opposite personalities of ourselves both in friendships and in marriage. That's how we balance each other and cause each other to grow. Tim is not only my husband but is also my friend. And we are opposites in many areas. Maybe in most areas! Sometimes, the different way we approach things can make us upset with each other. I tend to make decisions quickly; Tim likes to think things through. In my opinion, he sometimes takes too long. (Of course, in his opinion, I don't take enough time to weigh all the factors.) We've had some conflicts in this area, and we each have grown. I've learned to sometimes take more time to think things through. And he understands that some decisions need to be made quicker. It hasn't been easy to work through the conflict and talk it out, but we've both gained a better understanding of how the other person thinks and feels. It's caused us both to grow. I don't know why it often takes a problem to make us grow, but I find in my own life that I grow stronger by working through problems. And I believe our friendships will also grow stronger as we work through conflicts and hurts. It won't be easy or pain free. Most things of value aren't.

How can we talk through conflicts and hurts?

1. *Share your feelings with your friend in a nonthreatening way.* Use "I" statements. "I feel . . . because . . ." Without knowing it, we often put the other person on the defensive by the way we say things. For instance, Sharon has a problem with being late. Whenever Melody makes a date to get together with Sharon for lunch, dinner, or an outing, she finds herself waiting. And waiting. Sharon always has an excuse, but it makes Melody angry—angry enough to avoid even trying to get together with Sharon. If she went to Sharon and said, "You're always late every time we're supposed to get together," Sharon would feel attacked. Instead, Melody might say, "When you're late for lunch, I feel angry because we have so little time together. When you're late, our time is cut even shorter. I feel that maybe our time together isn't as important to you as it is to me."

Using "I" statements not only prevents putting the other person on the defensive, but it can help you to identify what you're really upset about. It can help your friend to understand why something is important to you. For Sharon and Melody, time together was important to Melody. Spending time together made her feel closer to Sharon. When Sharon

learned how important it was to Melody, she could understand why her lateness hurt Melody. Melody felt that the
friendship wasn't important to Sharon—otherwise, she
wouldn't be late.

2. Stick to the topic at hand. This isn't the time to bring
up past issues. Avoid saying such things as "You always . . ."
or "You never . . ."

3. Listen to the other person's side. Try to understand what
she is thinking and feeling. It may be helpful to "playback"
what you're hearing. After listening, put into your own words
what you think you heard the other person say and say it
back to her. "So what you're saying is . . ." Listen for her
feelings and try to identify them. "So you feel . . ." You may
not be right, but this will open the door for further discussion so that you both can understand how the other is feeling and what they're thinking. This will help you to understand what the conflict is all about. For Melody and Sharon,
Sharon's lateness had nothing to do with how Sharon felt
about her friendship to Melody. It had more to do with
Sharon's personality and tendency to over-schedule. As
Melody and Sharon worked through Sharon's lateness and
Melody's hurt, each could better understand the other.
Melody learned to expect Sharon to be late and not to take it
personally. Sharon realized how important time together was
with Melody and made more of an effort to be punctual.

4. Forgive your friend for the hurt. Forgive her even if she
doesn't ask for it. Not only will it likely heal the relationship,
but it will bring peace to your own heart. Without forgiveness, your heart will grow hard toward the one who has hurt
you, and there will be little hope for reconciliation. Say out
loud, "I forgive her for hurting me." Every time the devil
reminds you of what happened, say it aloud, "I've forgiven
her for that."

What if you don't want to forgive her? Then ask God to

give you the desire to do so. He will. He will help you to want to forgive your friend, and then He will enable you to forgive her.

5. *Remember that the goal of talking through the conflict is reconciliation, not victory.* This isn't the time or place to have to be right or to get your way. The goal is to work through the problem until both of you feel good about the solution— both of you. You haven't achieved reconciliation if one person walks away feeling good and the other person walks away still hurting. Don't stop the process until both of you agree that you feel the friendship has been restored.

6. *One of the best things you can do for your friendship and for the conflict or hurt is to pray together.* Praying together is one of the most strengthening things you can do with another person—even when there isn't a problem. Pray together as you begin talking through the problem, and then pray together when you feel the problem has been resolved. Ask God to guide you as you talk things through. Pray that He will keep your words kind and your motives pure and that He will protect feelings and help each person to be honest. Afterward, thank Him for guiding you through. Turn the friendship over to Him. Ask for His constant guidance and wisdom. Thank Him for your friend and all she means to you. Pray specifically for her and the needs in her life. It will mean so much to her to hear you pray specifically for her.

Instead of a hurt or conflict becoming a devastating experience, it can be a bonding time. It can actually strengthen your friendship instead of destroy it. How you deal with it makes the difference. It is hard to work through conflicts, to be honest and share how you feel. But your friendship will be so much richer and deeper for the effort. The pain is temporary; the joy more permanent.

One of the ways that many of us deal with conflict is to ignore it. We pretend it hasn't happened, or we avoid the person who has hurt us. I know that is my natural tendency! Too often, I find that when I've been hurt by a friend, I stay away from her, putting up walls so that she can't hurt me again. But these walls also prevent me from being a friend. I'm not talking with her. I neglect the little things, the little acts of kindness, that I would normally do. This can't continue very long without her feeling my coolness. And she may start pulling away too.

That's what happened between my friend and me in the situation described at the beginning of this chapter. She avoided me. She didn't return my calls and didn't appreciate my attempts at friendship. I didn't know what was going on. I tried to continue being a friend, but eventually the situation became so painful that I, too, started pulling away. The walls between us just continued to grow and grow.

Is that what God intends for friends? Especially Christian friends?

No. God tells us that if our brother (or sister) has something against us, we need to go to them and talk to them about it. And if we have something against our brother (or sister), we also need to go and talk to them about it. It was never God's intention for us to stuff our hurts and conflicts down inside us or for problems to destroy friendship. He has encouraged us—commanded us—to work through our problems with each other and, if necessary, to get help. He has told us to talk to the person with whom we have a problem, and if that doesn't help, to bring some godly people with us next time. Some conflicts may be so large that you will want the help of someone trained in conflict resolution. Begin by seeking the help of your pastor or spiritual leader of your congregation. If the problem requires the help of a counselor, be sure to find a Christian counselor who is grounded in God's Word.

God never wants us to allow walls to exist between ourselves and others. The Bible tells us that "a friend loves at all times" (Proverbs 17:17). It may be hard to love when you're hurting, but God can give you the strength and courage to love even when you feel incapable of it.

What happens if you've tried everything you can think of to heal the conflict and there's still no resolution? You've prayed about it. You've talked to your friend about it, sharing honestly with her how you feel. You've listened and clarified what you have heard her saying, trying to understand her point of view. You've forgiven her—even if she doesn't want forgiveness. But nothing has changed. The hurt and walls still loom large. What can you do?

If you've done everything you can, that's all you can do. It takes two to restore the friendship. If your friend doesn't want to forgive or isn't able to forgive, even though you've apologized sincerely and long for reconciliation, stay kind and loving toward her. Turn the situation over to God. It may take time before the friendship heals. It may never happen. Ask God to show you what to do and when. In *Can I Afford Time for Friendship?* Stormie Omartian writes: "If a friendship isn't to be restored, . . . we can count on God to give us a sense of peace one way or another about the friendships He brings into our lives."

When my friend was angry with me, I wanted very much to have the friendship restored. I tried to remain a faithful friend. Months later, when she was ready to talk about what she was feeling, I thought God was going to repair our friendship. I had prayed so long that healing would take place. We met and talked. We prayed together and cried together. I apologized, offering no excuses. I left thinking that we could begin our friendship again. But I was wrong. Even after talking and praying together, she couldn't get past the hurt. The walls never came down. Every time we found ourselves in the same room, it was painful. As I watched her talking with other friends and avoiding me, it hurt. There was nothing more I could do. I continued to turn the relationship over to God, but there was never healing. The friendship remains broken today.

That is not usually the case. When two friends come together with God, healing usually happens. But both friends have to want it. Both have to work for it. Both have to be willing to surrender their hurt and allow God to bring healing. Most of the time, the friendship will be stronger and the hearts bonded more deeply together.

That was the case with another friend when she bared her soul before me. She wasn't a close friend. But I admired her and was glad for the friendship we had. I looked forward to growing closer. Then she did something that hurt me and embarrassed me in front of a lot of people. I was devastated. As I look back, I realize now that I was too sensitive. I was so insecure I couldn't laugh at myself. Both she and I would handle the situation differently today. But we didn't then. I forgave her and let it go. We continued to be casual friends.

Then she did it again. This time it wasn't something that embarrassed me. In fact, it was so minor I didn't even realize what she had done. I totally forgot the whole incident for weeks—until I got a note from her in which she apologized for the incident. I had forgotten it and had never taken it personally! Due to my busy schedule, I failed to respond to her note. My silence made her think I was angry and hurt. (I hadn't given it a thought; I was just busy!) Her note shared her feelings honestly from her heart—her motives, thoughts, and jealousies. She bared her soul to me, asking my forgiveness. I was so drawn to her! To her honesty. I could relate to her feelings. They were feelings I had felt myself at other times. As a result of her note, I felt closer to her than I had ever felt before.

But she did more. She asked me to forgive her and to

remain friends, but said that she couldn't promise me that she would never do anything to hurt me again. More than likely, she admitted, she would end up being human and doing something hurtful. I loved her honesty! I knew then that she was someone with whom I wanted to have more than a casual friendship. Her honesty and openness had not only brought healing to our friendship (she was hurting over what she thought she had done) but had deepened it.

And she was right about the possibility of future hurts occurring. One of us probably will do something to hurt the other again. We need to expect that. We need to allow our friends to be human and fail us. And we need to be willing to forgive, seek healing, and go on. Sometimes it will take incredible courage and strength. It will always take God's love and guidance. But He is willing to help us. He's the God of reconciliation; He loves to restore relationships. He gave all He had to restore our relationship with Him, and He will give us what we need to restore our friendships with each other.

CHAPTER 6

How to Be There for a Hurting Friend

Naomi was hurting. A famine had left her country desolate, so she and her husband had moved from their homeland to find work and food. They packed up their belongings and two sons, said Goodbye to all their family and friends, and headed out, leaving the only life they had ever known. Naomi thought their new life would be better. In a strange land with new customs and among a people who didn't worship the God they knew, they attempted to settle down and make a prosperous life for the family.

But things didn't go well. Naomi's husband died. Then each of her sons died as well, leaving her alone with her sons' grieving widows. Maybe it was time to return home to the people she knew. But her heart was aching; she felt empty and alone. And bitter. Maybe she felt angry at God. How could He take everything from her?

The pain and loss clouded Naomi's eyes until she couldn't

see what she did have. She had Ruth. Ruth's name means "a woman friend." And Ruth was indeed a true friend. She promised Naomi unfailing love. She promised to stay by Naomi's side no matter what. Ruth left her own country and family behind to go with Naomi—a bitter Naomi who couldn't even acknowledge Ruth's presence. She followed Naomi to a strange land and a new God. To new customs and ways. She provided for Naomi's needs by working in the fields and gleaning what she could behind the harvesters.

Eventually Naomi realized what a treasure she had in Ruth. And the people around Naomi saw it too. They told her, "This Ruth is better to you than seven sons." Ruth had loved Naomi, cared for her, and stuck by her even when Naomi was miserable and couldn't do a thing to show Ruth love.

Sometimes when we are going through rough times, we're like Naomi. Sometimes pain so clouds our eyes that we can't see the people around us. We feel so needy ourselves that we think we have nothing to give. I know. I've been there.

When my father was dying, he and my mom were all I could think of. I was a needy person. Friends took care of my boys. One friend even took them to her house and kept them for several days. One day, my dad was fine. The next, he lay in an intensive care unit, more than an hour and a half away, unconscious, slowly slipping away from us. He had suffered a ruptured brain aneurysm. For eleven days his condition slowly worsened. The next days were spent preparing for the funeral and going through all of that. Our church stepped in and provided a meal. They served it and cleaned up afterward.

I remember getting a note from someone during that time—someone who didn't know what was going on in my life. She was a member of our church but no longer attended. I had periodically written to her, trying to keep in touch, trying to encourage her in her walk with the Lord and praying that she would come back. It had been awhile since I had written. In her note, she told me how much she missed my letters, how much they meant to her. I knew I should reply, but right then I just couldn't. I remember thinking, *I don't have anything to give.*

We all go through times when we don't have anything to give—when we need someone to take care of us but don't have anything to give in return. It's important during those times to allow people to help us. And that may mean asking for help. That is hard to do. At least, it is for me; I like to try to do things all myself. Yet I love helping other people. I'm blessed when I can help others. And we need to allow other people to receive that same blessing as they help us.

Sometimes our friends go through rough times—times when they need us. When they don't have anything to give. When we need to be a Ruth.

It may be tiring to keep giving and not be receiving anything back. You may need a listening ear or a friend yourself even as you find yourself in the midst of your friend's pain. But your friend may not have the strength to be there for you at that moment. That's one reason having more than one close friend is important. When you have two or three close friends, if one is hurting and in great need, you can give to them and find your needs met by another friend. If your friend is really hurting, she may not even be able to listen to you or your needs. That's when it's time to call another friend. But don't give up on the friend who is hurting. Hang in there. Continue to meet her needs and encourage her toward healing. One day, she'll be on the other side of her pain. Then your friendship can continue stronger than it was before. Look at Ruth and Naomi. Eventually, Naomi came through her pain, and when she was on the other side of it, you can be sure that she treasured Ruth more than she ever had before.

How can we be there for a hurting friend?

The two most important things we can do for our friends are to pray and to be there for them.

Praying for our friends doesn't mean only to pray *for* them, though that's very important. It's important to keep them before the throne of heaven in prayer, claiming promises and asking God to encourage them, comfort them, and surround them with His love. But it's also important to pray *with* our friends. Hearing someone pray for you brings courage, peace, and a feeling of being cared about. There's nothing that can bond a friendship stronger than praying together.

Recently a new friend called me. Her father had just died, and she was in the midst of making plans to travel out of state for the funeral. She talked to me about her dad dying. I could understand some of her feelings, since I had lost my own father a couple of years earlier. As we were ending our conversation, I asked her if I could pray for her. "That's why I called," she said. "I knew that you would pray for me." As we prayed, I asked the Holy Spirit to guide me in what to pray for. As we hung up in tears, we both sensed a love and care for each other—a closeness that strengthened our growing friendship. And I trust God that our prayer gave my friend strength and courage and the knowledge that someone cared.

It may seem awkward to you to pray with someone else, especially if praying out loud makes you nervous. Remember that prayer is something special between you and God. It doesn't matter if your words are awkward or if you don't know exactly what to pray for. God knows your heart. He hears your words through the love and care in your heart, and that makes your words beautiful to Him. It will also make your words beautiful to your friend. She won't care if you stumble over words or if you don't say exactly what you intend to. What she'll hear is your love intervening for her. That is what's really important. Don't let your awkwardness or fear stand in the way of blessing your friend through prayer.

Being there for a friend in the midst of her pain is also important. Sometimes we shy away from pain. We avoid friends who are in pain because we don't know what to say. "When Jared died an hour after he was born, it was the most devastating moment in my life," says Julia. "He was so perfect—his tiny fingers, his little toes. I held him for a long time, just breathing in his presence. We knew the moment he was born that he would die. I treasured those minutes with him. He changed my life even by his brief time. Afterward, few of my friends would talk to me about him. Few asked about him. They sent cards and flowers. They dropped off meals. And all those things were so helpful. But I wanted someone to listen to me. To let me tell them about Jared. To ask about him—'What color was his hair? Who did he look like?' He was my son. I'll never forget him. People still shy away when I try to talk about him. Maybe they're trying to spare me pain, but it hurts more to not talk about him. Then Karen came. She asked about Jared. 'What did he look like? Did he look like either of my other children?' I showed her the pictures and the snip of his hair the nurses gave me. She didn't say much; she just listened. She let me talk. That meant so much!"

When we don't know what to say, it's best to not say anything. But we can still show support by just being there and letting our friend talk—or by sitting in silence even if it does feel awkward. By your presence, let your friend know that you care. Be honest, tell your friend that you don't know what to say, but that you care. Hug her. Cry with her. Just be there for her.

"After George died, I felt so alone," Mary looks off in the distance before continuing. "No one came around. No one called. At the funeral everyone said they'd stop in, that they would call. But they haven't. It's just me. If they'd just stop by. Go for a walk with me or go out with me to dinner. I just need someone to talk with. I come home to an empty house with no one to tell what happened at work that day. The cat doesn't care. I need someone who does."

Many times, hurting friends just need someone to listen. To let them talk out what they're feeling. And let's face it; often when we feel we need to say something, we say something stupid: "It's for the best." "You're young; you can have another child." Such comments may be made with a sincere intention to comfort and help, but it's better to say nothing than to say something just to fill up the silence.

Instead, try to listen—really listen—to your friends. Try to draw them out and let them share their feelings. You can help by what my friend, Sue, calls "active listening." Active listening is not just listening to the words but hearing past the surface to what a person is really saying and feeling. The steps of active listening are the same steps that we looked at earlier when discussing how to resolve conflicts with friends.

As your friend shares her thoughts with you, replay back to her what you hear her saying. Gary Smalley calls this "Drive-through talking." It's what happens at the drive-through window of fast food restaurants. You place your order, and the order taker repeats it to you to make sure he has it right. In *Making Love Last Forever*, Smalley says, "Drive-through talking is when you say something to someone and you wait to hear it repeated back exactly the way you said it. If the other person gets it right—if he or she can tell you accurately what you just said without missing your meaning—you respond, 'Yes, you understand me.' If it isn't right, you say, 'No that's not what I said,' and you repeat the message until the individual gets it right."

We can listen to our friends in the same way. Listen to what they say and then repeat it back to them in your own words. They'll let you know if you've got it right. Listening this way helps to ensure that you understand what the other person is really saying. And it gives the other person the sense that he or she has been understood.

But there's more to what we say than our words. There are our feelings too. It's important to understand what your friend is feeling. As you listen to your friend, try to identify what she is feeling. Respond by sharing with her what you think you hear: "So what you're feeling is . . ." Again, she will let you know if you're right. If not, at least you will have opened the door for her to share with you what she is feeling.

When you replay back what your friend is saying and identify her feelings, your friend will feel that she has connected with you. That you understand what she feels and what she is going through. It will open the doors to deeper communication.

Active listening may seem phony at first. As I've listened actively to people, it has felt a little phony, even forced—as if I'm just going through steps. But active listening does make a difference. People will say, "Yes! That's exactly it!" And then they share more of what is happening in their lives.

As you listen to your friend, you may become aware of needs that you can meet in a practical way—a meal, a household chore, help with an errand or the children. These are important ways of helping a friend in pain. My first book, *How to Hug a Heart*, provides a lot of practical, simple ways to reach out to people in need. Through simple things such as sharing a pot of homemade soup or dropping off a take-out pizza, we can help another person and make him or her feel loved and cared about. Each person's needs will vary depending on his or her situation. Listening and watching will help you to determine things that need to be done.

When offering to help a friend, don't say "Let me know if there's anything I can do." No matter how sincere your offer, chances are your friend will never call you. Instead, offer to do something specific. "While we sit here and talk, I'm going to do your dishes. Where do you keep your dish detergent?" Don't ask your friend a question to which she can answer No. If you ask, "Can I do the dishes while we talk?" she will likely say "No, I'll get to them later." For most of us, it feels awkward to let someone else help us—even good friends.

If you truly don't know what to offer to do, and if you don't see anything that needs being done, ask God to show you if there is a practical way you can help. There have been times when I truly have not known how I could help. As Barb shared with me the pain she was experiencing in her life, I really didn't know how to help. I wanted to do something but had no idea what. So I told her honestly, "Barb, I really want to help, but I don't know how. Please let me know if there's anything I can do. I want to be there for you."

With tears Barb replied, "Invite me over. Ask me to come over for an afternoon. That would be nice."

If you can't think of anything to do, then let your friend know that you do truly want to help, but you just don't know how. Ask her if there's anything you can do. "I really want to help you through this, but I'm not sure what is the best way. How could I help you the most? What do you really need?" Then let her respond.

Sometimes our friends will push us away. Their pain causes them to withdraw into themselves. You may offer to help, and they might respond, "I'm OK. You already have so much to do. I'll be fine." You may need to be persistent in your offers of help, saying. "I don't have anything more important to do than to be here for you right now."

Dee Brestin writes, "In times of grief, we are apt to hear dark voices—voices that tell us we are no longer people of value, beloved by God. If we withdraw from friends, a common response to depression, then those voices have no competition.

We need to be with compassionate women who will come alongside us and show us that we are lovable human beings, precious in God's sight and in their sight." A hurting person needs her friends, even when she thinks she doesn't.

Naomi tried to push Ruth away. She told her to go home. Basically she said, "You're better off without me. Go home. Have a life. I have nothing to offer you." But Ruth was persistent. She stuck by Naomi despite the way Naomi treated her. We may need to be persistent like Ruth and stick by our friend no matter what—even if her words and actions are hurtful to us. I often remind my boys that "hurting people hurt people." A person in pain often causes pain to others. Naomi's words, and later her silence, may have hurt Ruth. But Ruth's love was faithful. Ruth knew what Naomi was really like. She knew that the pain Naomi was feeling was causing Naomi to act and respond the way she did. We, too, need to remember that hurting people may cause us pain. The Bible says, "A friend loves at all times" (Proverbs 17:17)—even during difficult times when your friend isn't fun to be around.

As we watch our friends go through painful experiences, we will naturally want them to reach the other side. But remember to give your friend the time she needs to grieve. There is no proper time to get over a major hurt or tragedy. The time for grieving will be different for each person. Some people may come through quickly; others may take longer. Our goal is to walk alongside, encouraging, but not pushing, our friend to continue toward healing.

At the same time, we don't want to allow our friend to wallow in her pain—to immerse herself in the hurt and not continue on to the other side. We need to ask God for wisdom and discernment to know the proper balance between pushing and allowing our friend to wallow in pain.

If a friend seems stuck in her pain, we can gently nudge her on. Encourage her to get out. Invite her to lunch. Encourage her to talk about the pain and engage in active listening with her, helping her to face it. Ask her what it would take to help the healing process. In some cases, a friend may need to seek professional counseling. And we may need to confront her, asking her what she is doing to move toward healing. If it comes to that, confrontation always needs to be done in love, never in judgment—and then only after much prayer and listening in order to understand what she is thinking and feeling.

Painful experiences happen to all of us, and they come in many different ways. Miscarriage. Death. Illness. Divorce. Depression. A lost job. Financial problems. An accident. A difficult relationship. It may even be something that others consider minor. But whatever it is, God desires for us to "bear one another's burdens" (Galatians 6:2). I think that's one reason He gave us friends—to help us through the difficult times of life. To be His love to each other.

When my dad died, my friends truly loved me with God's love. Tanya called me daily to make sure I was OK. I could tell her what I was feeling—my fears, the pain. Talking with her helped me to be strong when I was going to the hospital with my mom every day and then later when I had to help with the funeral arrangements. Beverly took care of the meal for the funeral. She arrived at Mom's early the morning of the funeral with coolers and ice and food. She had everything ready to serve when family and friends arrived afterward. And she stayed till everything was cleaned up. Lilly took care of my boys during the last few days before Dad died, keeping them day and night. She was there when I received the call that Dad had died. Donna helped with the boys during the viewing and took Zachary home with her after the funeral. Mary brought me a bouquet of dried flowers a few weeks after the funeral. Each saw a need and helped in the way they could. Each helped to ease the pain a little and showered God's love on me a lot.

That's what friends are for.

CHAPTER 7

Drawing Friends to Christ

She hadn't been to church in years. She had gone because her parents made her, because it was expected. She wasn't sure she had ever had a real relationship with Jesus. But she struggled with religion's role in her life and where it would fit. When she found herself pregnant and unmarried, she knew for sure the people at her church wouldn't have time for her. That they would walk away from her and ignore her. That they would condemn her.

She was surprised at how they responded. One woman gave her maternity clothes she no longer needed. Another invited her to lunch—just to talk, not to lecture or condemn. She and Paula got together often. Paula never preached, just listened and gave advice when asked. Then the church really surprised her with a baby shower. She hadn't expected that. She knew what she had done was wrong, but the women of the church responded with such love. The ladies had surrounded her as the shower came to a close and prayed for her, for her baby, for their future.

"Paula, why are they doing this for me?" she asked at the shower, through tears.

Paula smiled and put her arm around the young woman, "Because they love you."

"But I've done so many bad things," she protested.

"We've all done wrong things. That doesn't make us un-lovable. God sent His Son to die for us *while* we were sinners. He knew that we would sin, but He loved us anyway. And He wants us to love others with His love. That's what's happening here. These ladies are loving you with God's love." Paula watched the young girl and prayed. All the women in the church had been praying. When they had found out one of their teens was pregnant and unwed, they had come together and talked. "How can we help? What can we do?" They had decided to love her with God's love—and to pray. They had been praying for her, for her baby, and for her salvation every day.

"Do you think God still loves me?" Her voice was trembling. But Paula knew the moment was ripe. The women in the room noticed as Paula and the young woman went to a quiet part of the room. Silent prayers were lifted as the two knelt in prayer together. The women's hearts rejoiced; they knew God had won the victory. They had prayed and reached out with love, and God had answered.

Cami longs for her friend to know Jesus. But April has told her she wants no part of God or church. Her voice held a slight twinge of bitterness as she told Cami about hurts she had experienced in the past. "When my son died, I was vulnerable. I needed someone to care. But no one from the church called or visited. I know I didn't attend often. But they all knew that he had died. If one of them had reached out to me, maybe then . . ." Cami tries to convince April to give the church and God another chance. "He wasn't there for me when Nathan died," April tells her. "Neither were His people. I don't know that they would be now either." Cami continues to pray.

Delores longs for her neighbor, Christine, to know Jesus. They enjoy walking together each morning. Debbie has been praying for years that her daughter would come back to the Lord. Peggy has been witnessing to a woman at work with whom she has developed a friendship during the long hours they have spent working together. She knows that her co-worker would find peace and strength to face her struggles if she knew Christ.

Each of us have people we love—friends, family, neighbors, even people in our churches—whom we long to see come to Jesus. They need to know that God loves them and that He desires to be actively involved in their lives. We pray for their salvation. Maybe we enlist others to pray too. Our hearts ache for them, yet sometimes we don't know exactly what to do. How can we draw our friends to Christ? How did He draw people to Himself?

Jesus prayed for people. He took time each day to talk with His Father. He prayed for those He was ministering to and for those in the future who would believe (that's us!). He prayed for God to soften their hearts, to allow them to hear the words He shared.

Prayer is the most important thing we can do for a friend. But sometimes it feels as though we pray so long and nothing happens. We keep praying for their salvation but see no results.

I prayed for my mom for fourteen years. Every day I prayed that God would draw her to Him, that she would find salvation in Him. I begged. I pleaded. There were days that I prayed with tears streaming down my face. But time kept going by, and nothing happened. Then, after fourteen years of my prayers, Mom was baptized into the church I belong to. Did God wait fourteen years and then answer my prayer? Did He say, "Well, Tami has been praying a long time. I guess it's time to answer her prayers"?

No! Looking back, I can see how God was leading my mom step by step during all that time. First, He gave her a desire to seek Him. She tried the churches my brothers attend, but neither seemed to fill the longing in her heart. So I invited her to mine. She agreed to come for a month. The month stretched into a year. She attended Bible studies, retreats, seminars, and small groups.

When our church held a series of evangelistic series, she came—"for only two or three nights," so she said. Instead, she *missed* only two or three nights, and she missed these only because of snow. She was among the first to be baptized. It was a time of incredible rejoicing for me.

It's been four years since my mom was baptized. This spring, she returned from her third mission trip to the Dominican Republic. She had even taken Spanish classes over the winter so she could communicate better. Watching her grow has been a joy. The growth has come in steps, too, just like God drew her to Him.

Praying for someone's salvation is a goal. It may take a while for the person we are praying for to reach the goal for which we are praying, but God is working all along—step by step. We can pray in steps too. Pray for little things that will lead to salvation. This will help us see God's hand as He leads our friend to Him. God loves to answer our prayers. He loves for us to see answers to prayer. Not only can we pray for the salvation of someone we care about, but we can also pray each day for something new that we believe God can do; we can pray for Him to move our friend a step closer toward salvation.

Christine was a woman I barely knew. She had attended

our church for a while. Her life wasn't easy. She had made difficult choices and was having to live with them. I passed her home every day, and each time I did so, I prayed for her salvation and that God would give her a desire for Him. I knew that I needed to do more, that I needed to stop and let her know that I cared. That God cared. So one morning as I passed her home, I prayed, "God, give me the courage to stop and knock on her door—or cause me to run into her. Please do something so that I can see her and let her know that You love her."

That afternoon I ran into Christine at the store. That very afternoon! I knew that God had arranged it. So with courage from Him, I went up and talked with her. I'll never forget what she said when I invited her to come back to church. "I've been wanting to," she responded. God had given her the desire. That was the first step. The second step was causing our paths to meet. That week, Christine and her children came to church. I can't tell you what joy it was to see her walk through those doors! I knew that God was working.

A woman I know was praying for her friend's salvation. I suggested to her that in addition to praying for her friend, she should begin praying for steps toward that salvation. What steps did she believe God could bring about? What would it take for her friend to turn to God? I reminded her that God loves to show us that He is answering our prayers. Answered prayers remind us that God is listening and of His love and power. She decided to give it a try and began praying that her friend would recognize God's intervention in his life.

That week she called me; she was very excited. It seems her friend's car had broken down in the middle of a busy city. Someone stopped to help who had exactly what he needed—a funnel and water! He knew this had to be God at work. Not many people carry a funnel in the car. He recognized that God had sent just the right person at just the right time with just the right tools to help. He hasn't yet decided to surrender his life to Christ, but he's beginning to believe that God does care for him—personally. And it's given my friend more courage and determination in praying for him. She sees God working and believes He will answer her prayers. And He has begun to do so. By praying for steps toward salvation, she is seeing God working toward her friend's salvation.

How do you pray steps? Think about what it would take for God to bring your loved one to the place of surrender and salvation. What needs to happen? Why hasn't your loved one come to Christ? What do you believe God could do?

Now, I know that God can do anything; nothing is impossible for Him. But it's easier to believe that in theory than to put it to the test. Pray specifically. Then when God answers, you will see it. Seeing God answer our prayers gives us courage and hope.

For a long time, I've been praying for a couple I love. I long to see them growing in a relationship with God. I know that He could make such a difference in their lives. But there have been a few obstacles. Their friends aren't Christian. They hang out with people who love to party. Both of them drink and smoke. The husband attended church as a teenager, but his wife has never attended. She's not sure she even believes there is a God.

What steps could I pray as I pray for their salvation?

First, that God would bring them godly friends—and that He will help me to be such a friend (never pray a prayer unless you're willing to be part of the answer). They need to have friends who love the Lord and whose lives will be a witness to Him. Second, I prayed that they would have a distaste for alcohol and the lifestyle that goes with it. Then I prayed that the wife would see God as real in her life.

God has been answering. Both have stopped drinking, and they've told their friends who drink to not come around anymore. They want to change their lives. The man has gotten a new job with a boss who seems to really care. I don't know if he's a Christian or not, but he definitely is taking care of my friend. Then the wife got a new job, too—a job at a place where I know there are many Christians working. Will God open friendships there? I believe He will. And the most exciting answer to prayer was the evening the woman started asking questions: "How do you know God is real?" "How can you believe that the Bible is true?" God is working on her heart. The Holy Spirit is leading her. Seeing God specifically leading and answering my prayers gives me hope and courage to persevere and to believe that one day soon this man and his wife will come to God completely.

While you're praying for your friend and spending time with her, it doesn't hurt to ask her what in her life you can pray for. Most people will mention something. And then remember to follow through and pray. Remind your friend, when you see her, that you're praying. As God works in answers to your prayer, and she sees those answers, it will be another way of drawing her to Christ.

Christ not only prayed for people; He also met their needs. He gave them food and healed them. He talked to them with respect and love. The Gospels are full of stories of His touch on other people's lives. He's given us an example to follow.

While you continue to pray for your friends, you can meet needs in their lives and show them your love—and God's love through what you do. I know that my mom was drawn to God as she saw people recognizing and meeting needs in her life. When my brother died, my parents were devastated. He was the baby of the family; a senior in high school. On his way home from work one night, he was killed by a drunk driver. Mom had just come home from the hospital the day before the accident. She had had surgery on her ankle and couldn't get around very well.

Christian friends came and helped. They brought casseroles and pies. They came to the viewing despite a snowstorm that hit that very evening. Many members of our church drove an hour one way to come and pay condolences for a young man they didn't really know. A lot of family members didn't brave the storm. It impressed my parents that the people from my church would come so far and bring food and send cards and notes. This was one of the first steps toward softening their hearts to what I believed and to the people I worshiped with. They had felt their love and seen it in action.

Carol had met Charlie at the fitness club. They talked often while they exercised. Carol felt a burden to share Christ with Charlie and had been praying for an opportunity. "I really felt drawn to Charlie. Our lives were very different. She was moving up the corporate ladder, dating one guy after another. I worked part time and had three kids. I've been married to the same man for seventeen years. Despite our differences, I really liked Charlie. She was fun and smart. She thought it was nice that I went to church and said that someday when she had kids, maybe she'd go. But she didn't have time for that right now. I wanted so much for her to see how God loved her. How He could be a part of her life right now."

Then Charlie didn't show up at the fitness club for several nights in a row. Carol grew concerned and decided to stop by her apartment to make sure everything was OK. She found Charlie at home with the flu. She was miserable, and the apartment was a wreck. Carol straightened up and made some soup before heading home. The next day, she stopped by again, bringing supper and a few groceries. Every day,

Carol stopped by. She did some laundry or washed dishes or fixed supper until Charlie was feeling better.

"Why did you do this for me?" Charlie asked. She liked Carol and considered her a friend, but none of her other friends had ever done anything like this for her. She was overwhelmed by Carol's love. Their friendship grew, and Charlie began finding herself at Carol's home in the evenings, eating dinner and playing games with Carol's kids. She watched as the family prayed together before meals and had family worship in the evening.

"I want whatever it is that you have," Charlie told Carol one evening. It wasn't long before Charlie was coming to church with Carol's family. As the church family reached out to her, too, through smiles, conversation, and invitations to lunch, Charlie began to grow spiritually. She wanted to have a relationship with the God who had made these people so caring.

Tears streamed down Carol's face as Charlie was baptized. Charlie shared with the church how God had led her to Him. She said, "Carol never preached a word. She just showed me that she loved me through her actions. She always cared about what was happening in my life. She listened to what I said—really listened. And she took care of me when I was sick. It was love that drew me."

Saint Francis of Assissi once wrote something to this effect: "Preach the gospel, and if you must, use words." Even without words, we can share God's love through our actions. By meeting needs in people's lives, we will speak volumes about our care and concern. Sometimes those needs will be for a smile or a listening ear or a hug. Meeting needs may sometimes require more. It may mean sharing a meal or lending a helping hand. People will see God's love in us as we love them through Him. (For more ideas on how to make a difference in someone's life through small kindnesses, read

How to Hug a Heart.)

Jesus prayed for people, and He met their needs. Then He shared God with them. He taught them what God was like and told them how great God's love was for them. First, He showed them the Father's love through His interaction with them—through His words and by meeting their needs—then He was able to tell them about the Father, and they were willing to listen to Him. Why? Because they knew He cared.

God will open the doors for us to share Him with others, especially as we befriend people, loving them with His love, meeting their needs, and being there for them. When we are meeting needs is not the time to preach. The most effective way of sharing Christ with others is to tell what He's doing in our own lives. Of the women surveyed, almost all said that their friends drew them closer to God by sharing with them what God was doing in their own lives. How He was working. The little ways they saw evidences of His love in their lives.

Sharing what God is doing for you can be natural if He's a natural part of your life. If you're used to watching for glimpses of Him everyday, it'll be natural to share them with a friend. I've heard that more people are won by testimonies than by preaching. As you share testimonies of Jesus, big and small, you will be winning others for Him. It will make God real and show that He is a God who is caring and involved in the lives of His people.

Sharing what Jesus has done for you can make a lasting impression. During our church service, we have a praise and testimony time. Between songs, people are invited to share a praise or testimony of God. This is a favorite part of our worship service. Wanda once told how one Friday evening she and her son were walking through town. She was feeling a little discouraged. As a single mom, the load she carried was heavy at times. When they came to the town square, a choir was performing. She and her son sat and listened. The music lifted her spirits and changed her attitude. When the concert came to a close, she realized that she and her son were the only ones who had stopped to listen; everyone else had kept on walking. "I knew that God had provided a concert just for me," she declared. "He knew I was discouraged and wanted to lift my spirits." Wanda shared this testimony almost two years ago, but I still remember it. And it moves my heart to know that God loves us that much. That He cares about our feelings and arranges things just for us.

As you spend time with your friends who don't know God, help them to know Him—to learn what kind of God He is—by sharing what He's doing in your life. Did He protect you somehow this week? Did He provide something for you when you needed it? Or when you didn't need it, but wanted it? How did He show you that He loved you? What makes His love real to you? What makes Him real to you? How is God working in your life? How do you see evidences of His love?

In order to share with others about God, you first need to have a relationship with Him. You have to see and believe that He's changing you, that He loves you, before you can convince anyone else that He is worth making time for in their lives.

If you're not seeing God at work in your life, pray and ask Him to open your eyes to the evidences of His power and love. Sometimes we get so busy we lose our connection with Him, and we miss out on seeing Him. But He will willingly help us see Him at work.

Help your friends see how God is working in their lives too. Kim and I are studying the Bible together. I'm praying that our time together will draw Kim to God. One week, Kim told me how she had locked herself out of her car earlier in the week. She wasn't in a great section of town and didn't know what to do. A man came by and asked if he could help her. He was big and dressed in jeans and a T-shirt with a bandanna tied around his head. But Kim never felt afraid. "He was so nice. And He knew how to unlock my car without keys. I was on my way in just a couple of minutes."

I instantly saw it as God working and told her so. "God really took care of you. I wonder if the guy was an angel."

"Do you think it could have been an angel?" Kim's eyes were big as she thought about it. It was natural for me to recognize God's protection and provision. I look for it daily in my own life, and I pray that He will open my eyes to Him. I long for Kim to see God working in her life, too, because He is! God is at work in each of our lives. And I wouldn't be surprised if the man who helped Kim was an angel. To me, that's the kind of God we have—a God who takes care of His people however and whenever He can.

As you share God, naturally and openly, your friend may have questions about Him and about what you believe. Then it's time to offer to study the Bible with them. (This is a step you can pray for—that your friend will desire to study the Bible.) It's important to find the right Bible study. Many studies are doctrinal; they teach what the church believes. These types of studies are geared for someone who already has a relationship with Jesus and wants to understand what you believe. But they aren't good for someone who doesn't know God in a personal way. Instead, find a Bible study that teaches what a personal relationship with Jesus is all about, such as the seven-lesson study "Come Alive With Jesus," available from Hart Research Center. Each lesson covers a simple, basic aspect of our Christian walk—what it means to become a Christian, how to study and pray and grow, learning to share with others, and the importance of fellowship with other believers.

As you study each lesson with your friend, share incidents from your own experience. When you talk about what it means to accept Jesus as your Savior, share how you came to the place of giving your life to Him and what it has meant to you. As you talk about Bible study and prayer, share what you have found meaningful for your life in these areas. If there are things that have helped you to grow or to understand the Bible better or to pray in a way that felt meaningful, share them. Reading a lesson is one thing, but hearing how it really works in another person's life makes it real— and possible. It causes people to think, "If God did that in your life, then maybe He'll do it for me."

Can we make a difference in the lives of our friends? Can we lead our friends to Christ?

As we follow Christ's example of praying for our friends— not only for their salvation but praying specifically, step by step, meeting their needs, listening to them, hugging them, taking care of them, and sharing with them how God works in our life, helping them to see how He's working in theirs, and, if possible, sharing God's Word with them through Bible study—we will see our friends come to Christ.

Eva and Josie had been friends since high school. They shared everything. Till Eva became a Christian. "When I started dating Jon, I knew there was something special about him and his family," Eva says. "There was a closeness, a sense of happiness. They told me that God had made the difference in their lives. It wasn't long before I was attending church with them. I accepted Jesus as my Savior and was baptized. What an incredible day! I felt so new and clean. But Josie didn't understand. As God changed my life, Josie watched but just couldn't understand. She kept saying, 'Don't talk to me about God. If you need this religion thing, fine. But I'm OK.' I longed for her to experience Jesus as I have."

Eva began praying for Josie. She remained a real friend.

She didn't allow their different beliefs to change how she felt about Josie. She chose to love Josie and be her friend even if Josie never became a Christian. "She was just too important to me." Eva says. We'd been through so much. I had new friends who did share my love of Jesus. They gave me strength and courage—and prayed for Josie. I still made sure we did things together. And I tried to be there for her."

Josie was resistant at first, but slowly Eva began seeing changes. Josie began listening more and asking questions. "At first, when I'd share something God had done during my day, Josie didn't seem to believe it was God. She'd just smile and change the subject. Then from time to time she'd share something that happened in her life. She never said it was God, but I could see she was beginning to wonder if it could be."

Eva started including Josie in activities—fun things— with her friends from church. "My church has a ladies' night out. We all meet at a restaurant and have dinner together. Nothing is planned; we just talk and have fun. I invited Josie to come and she said Yes. She got to know some of the other ladies and seemed to have a fun time."

Today, Josie and Eva worship in the same church. Josie was baptized several years after Eva's baptism. She says that Eva's friendship is what brought her. "Eva never preached. That would've turned me off," Josie says today. "She just lived this life that—I don't know, she was so peaceful and had such joy. Her friends did too. And they were real. Not perfect. When she talked about God, she made Him sound so real. I started seeing things in my own life and wondering if it could be God. Eventually I knew that I needed what she had. I wanted a relationship with this God who gave her such joy. It's been incredible."

It *is* incredible to have a personal relationship with a God who loves us so intimately and completely. And it's even more incredible to see our friends coming to know Him and to be a part of helping them find Jesus. A study showed that 57 percent of adults joining the church listed family and friends as the most important influence in their decision for baptism.[*]

Is there someone God longs to reach through you?

[*] Monte Sahlin, *Sharing Your Faith With Your Friends Without Losing Either* (Hagerstown, Md.: Review and Herald Publishing Association, 1990), 50.

CHAPTER 8

Iron Sharpening Iron

It's fun to get together with friends. The social aspect of friendship is very important. We all need to have people to do things with. God created us with a need to belong, to be a part of people. He created us for companionship with Him. He longed to walk and talk with us. And He is a God of fun. Just look at all He created. When I see animals playing, otters for example, I know that God delights in laughter and fun. He definitely didn't want life to be boring.

God also created friends so we could bear one another's burdens and encourage one another. He knew life would be tough, and He wanted us to know that we aren't alone. That He's there for us—sometimes through the words and hugs of a friend.

But to me, one of the most exciting aspects of friendship is how it helps me grow. Proverbs 27:17 says, "As iron sharpens iron, so one [woman] sharpens another" (NIV). God desires our friendships to strengthen us. To cause us to grow. He knows what friendship can do for us, how it can make us stronger. God knows that friendships can teach us to be better people, and most importantly, that they can help us grow in Him.

I have several friends who have definitely sharpened me, helping me to grow stronger and more confident, more secure. Friends help me reach my dreams and rejoice with me when my dreams come true. I know that each of them would give the praise to God; that's the way they are. And I know that it's been God who has truly changed me and helped me grow. Many times, however, He has caused those changes and that growth to come about through the influence of friends.

One of the friendships that has given me the most strength and courage is my friendship with Sue. Sue and I have been friends for a long time. She's always been special to me. But four years ago, we made a decision that has changed both of us tremendously. We decided to become prayer partners. We made a promise to meet once a week for an hour to talk, share, and pray. And we've been keeping that promise ever since. We meet at her office each Thursday morning at eleven o'clock. Her boss lets us use a conference room. During the summer, we meet at the church, which is only five minutes from Sue's office. That way my boys can skateboard in the parking lot, and Sue and I can have privacy to talk and pray. If something comes up and Thursday doesn't work, we're committed to meeting another day.

Our time together isn't limited to Thursdays. We talk on the phone throughout the week, and sometimes we do things together as well. Sue is one of the people I want to call first when something happens—good or bad. But it's been our weekly prayer hour that has been the catalyst for everything else.

What do we do during this hour that has changed us?

We talk and pray. That sounds simple—and it is. But it's more than just talking about day-to-day things. Seven key things about our prayer time make it special.

The first is transparency—the ability to share absolutely anything and to be completely honest. When we get together, Sue and I talk about our past week and future plans. We share the ways God has blessed us. We also confess bad attitudes and motives, as well as areas we've failed and areas we've struggled with. We open our hearts.

Transparency doesn't happen instantly. It's a process. It comes slowly, as you share and find that your friend is trustworthy. As transparency develops, you are willing to share more. The trust you share isn't just trusting that your friend won't tell anyone the private things you share with her. It's a trust that she will still love you and not condemn you.

And that's the second key element to the time Sue and I spend together—unconditional love and a nonjudgmental attitude. When I was discussing this chapter with Sue, I listed the different things I felt were important between friends who wanted to strengthen and sharpen one another. Sue said that the unconditional love that exists between us—the knowledge that no matter what we share with each other, we will still be friends and love each other—was one of the most important things. Such love is a key to being able to be transparent with each other.

When a friend confesses a fault or a struggle, she is making herself vulnerable. She knows that she is involved in something wrong and that she needs to change. She needs a friend who will love her and help her through to victory. When friends share such situations with me, I can often relate to what they're confessing. After all, I'm a sinner too!

Cassie confided to me that she felt jealous when her friend Maria was promoted to vice president of her company. Cassie was in a similar field and was striving for a new position too. But she confided more than her jealousy. She told me how she tried to find things wrong with Maria and point them out. It made her feel a little better—for a time. I could understand. There have been times when I've felt jealous of a friend's accomplishment and haven't responded the way I should. Have you?

I'm not saying we should condone the wrong or say "That's OK." That's not how Sue responds to me! She'll say, "You're right! That is a wrong attitude. Have you talked to God about it? What do you think He wants you to do?" She's neither condemning me nor condoning my behavior. She's pointing me to God and accepting me as a person. That's why I can share things with Sue that I wouldn't share with anyone else. I've learned that she's trustworthy. That she can know me—the good and the bad—and still love me. She may not always like how I act or what I do or say, but she will always love me.

Accountability is another key element to our friendship. Accountability is so important, and it's missing so often today. Each of us is doing our own thing; we're on our own, spiritually and emotionally, in our thoughts and in what we do.

When I was a teenager, my youth leader always asked me the same question every time I saw him. Even when I was older and visited Jim with my new husband, Jim's first question was still the same, "How are you and God doing?" It wasn't just a rote question; it was something Jim honestly cared about. He cared about my relationship with God, and he wanted to know where I was spiritually. He made me accountable. He counted on me to answer honestly.

That's how we make our friends accountable. We ask them direct questions that pertain to the areas of their lives about which they want to be accountable or need to be. Your friend may have specific areas for which she wants you to hold her accountable. And you may have areas in your life for which you want her to hold you accountable too. I appreciate how my friends help me in this area.

Often when Tanya and I talk, we'll ask each other, "What have you been doing to take care of yourself lately?" We both are stay-at-home moms with children; we both have two boys. We're both involved in the church and other activities. Our lives are busy, and one of the first things that gets pushed aside in our full schedules is time for ourselves. Time to read a book or take a bubble bath or go for a walk. We both know how important that quiet time is for us. Without it, we can become grumpy, frazzled, and less than the best moms we could be. We need to take time to renew ourselves so we have more to give to our families and to our responsibilities.

Tanya and I also encourage one another to spend time with our husbands. We know that this is important for our marriages. We trade off baby-sitting, so we can each have a "date" with our husbands. If one of us hasn't spent some time alone with our husband in a while, the other will ask, "When are you going to let me watch the boys so you guys can go out?" We haven't actually said, "Let's help keep each other accountable about spending time with our husbands." It's something that has come about naturally. We know what's important to each other. We know that the most important thing to each of us is our families—our sons and our husbands. And because we love each other, it's easy for us to ask these important questions naturally. We want the very best for one another. Holding each other accountable in the areas that mean the most to our lives is our way of showing that we care; it's our way of taking care of each other.

Time management is tough for me. There are so many good things to be involved in, and I have a hard time saying No to any of them! I love being busy. My husband can't understand that; he likes one thing at a time. My schedule overwhelms him. But there are times when I'm too busy even for myself. So I need friends who love me to help hold me accountable in my use of time. When I'm offered something new to do, Sue will ask, "How does this fit what God wants you to do? Is this something God wants you to do or just another thing to use up your time?"

Sue knows that while I enjoy being involved in a variety of

activities, more importantly, I want to be involved in the things God wants me to do. She knows that I don't want to do anything—no matter how wonderful it would be—unless God has asked me to be a part of it. Sue holds me accountable by reminding me to look to God before taking on anything else. Sue's personality is more like Tim's. She often says, "You make me tired just listening to what you're doing." But she knows I enjoy it, and she sees how God is working in my life. She never tells me I shouldn't be involved in something; that's not for her to judge. She just points me to the One who will guide me and show me how to spend my time. Psalm 31:15, NKJV, says, "My times are in Your hand." That's what both Sue and I want.

Recently Sue was asked to lead a committee at church. I knew she would do a great job; she's got a lot of gifts and talents. But after praying about it, Sue felt that she needed to say No. She had just taken on a responsibility in a ministry outside of our local church that was important to her and felt she couldn't do both. She felt bad saying No (we're learning to say No together). I encouraged her in her answer. "You're right for saying No, Sue. God has called you to this other job. You don't have time for both. God has someone else to lead this committee. You need to follow His leading."

Taking on another task sometimes feels easier than saying No. Why do we feel so guilty saying No? If God wants something done, He'll get it done. We need to trust Him. Not only do Sue and I hold each other accountable regarding the time we give projects, but we encourage one another as we follow God's leading. If the other person needs to say No, we make sure we let her know that she has made the right decision. We back each other up.

Another area of accountability is in using and developing spiritual gifts. Look for your friend's gifts and talents. Encourage her to use those gifts and hold her accountable for using them. Ask, "How are you using this gift for God?" If God has given you a gift or talent, He's blessed you with it so that you can use it for Him. A friend recently told me of her desire to do something for God, but she wasn't sure what. She didn't feel she could get up front and speak, and going door to door sharing Jesus with strangers frightened her. This friend is gifted artistically. As I prayed with her, I asked God to open the door for her to use her artistic talent for Him. The thought that perhaps God could use her art and creativeness to bring Him glory was a new one for her. God can, and I believe He will. I've already seen Him working through her as she's made beautiful flower arrangements for our church—a different one for every season. They decorate our sanctuary and remind us of the beauty of God.

Not only can you ask your friend how she's using her gifts for God, you can help her to see what her gifts are and to find ways to use them. No matter what our talents and abilities, God can use them to draw people closer to Him.

Sue and I hold each other accountable in a lot of areas of our lives by asking each other questions during our time together. Because staying healthy is important to both of us, we ask each other, "How are you doing with exercising and eating?" And sometimes we both have to admit that we're doing awfully. (As I sit here, I can't remember the last time I went for my morning walk; it must have been a week already!) There are times when we both have been doing great too. Or one of us is, and the other isn't. We don't get angry when the other asks us these questions; it's not prying or an attempt to make the other person live up to certain expectations or to judge her if she isn't doing well. If one of us is having trouble doing well in an area— or if both of us are—we just pray that God will guide us.

Because both of us are writers, we also ask each other, "How are you doing with your writing?" We both teach Sabbath School—Sue in primaries, I in juniors. "How are you doing with Sabbath School?" often sparks new ideas for our own classes as the other shares things she is doing with her kids.

As we talk, each of us keeps a list of the things the other has mentioned or asked prayer for. That way we can follow up the next week when we're together again. If one of us shares a struggle or situation one week, the other will ask her about it the next time we're together. That encourages us to grow—especially when it involves an area in which we are weak or that is a sin. We know the other person is going to ask us how things are going, and we want to be able to report good news.

Irene and Shirley are prayer partners and friends. They've learned to be transparent with each other and to show unconditional love. When Irene told Shirley that she was feeling attracted to a man at work, Shirley held Irene accountable to doing what God would want. Irene was married. She and her husband worked different shifts and didn't see each other often. Certain things about her husband irritated Irene; the man at work was always nice and pleasant. He paid special attention to Irene—complimenting her and bringing her small gifts. Irene looked forward to having him stop by her office. She enjoyed their conversations. Soon she found herself looking forward to seeing the man at work more than she looked forward to going home. She knew it was wrong. Part of her wanted to end it, but another part didn't. The man at work made her feel special.

Irene was able to share her feelings with Shirley because she knew she could trust her. Shirley wouldn't tell anyone nor would she judge Irene. She prayed with Irene about the situation. Irene knew what she needed to do, and Shirley held her accountable by asking her how things were going and by pointing her to what God wanted her to do. First, they prayed that Irene would have a desire to let go of the situation. Then they prayed that God would work things out. The man was suddenly transferred to another department, but God wasn't finished yet. Things worked out so that Irene and her husband worked the same shift and had more time together. Renewing their friendship with each other was top priority. Shirley prayed with Irene all through the situation, asking the tough questions and standing by her friend.

I've had friends who have had to hold me accountable in tough areas. With the love that only a close friend has, they have pointed out sin in my life and have held me accountable for changes I needed to make. When Janet pointed out a wrong attitude in my life, I knew she wasn't condemning me. I knew I could trust her love. She told me flat out, "That's sin." But it didn't end there; she prayed with me that God would give me the desire and courage to change. And then she kept checking in on me to see how things were going.

Being accountable to someone else helps you to grow. You can't just coast along or stay where you are. You know that someone is going to be asking how you're doing and that they will be asking because they love you and want to see you reach your full potential in God.

We've looked at the following keys to sharpening one another as you interact with your friends—being transparent, loving unconditionally, and holding each other accountable. The next key is dreaming dreams for your friend.

When I think about this key, I think of Janet. Janet has been dreaming bigger dreams for me than I could ever dream possible for myself. Tucked in my Bible is a note she wrote me many years ago. Janet had invited me to share a testimony at camp meeting, and I had said No. Then I felt bad that I had refused. She wrote, "Don't feel bad. There will be many more opportunities. I believe God has a lot of appointments ahead for you." At the time, I had spoken in my community at local churches, but I couldn't imagine God asking me to be a speaker. It wasn't a part of my dreams. Janet dreamed it for me. And God has opened doors. He's given me the opportunity to speak to people across the country. It's been fun and exciting; it's so incredible to see God at work.

Janet has also dreamed dreams for me regarding writing. As I finished writing my first book, she was already asking about the next one. I wasn't sure there would even be a next one. When the second book was released, I received an e-mail from Janet. She had renamed me; my new name was the name of a popular author I admire—June Strong. I had met her briefly at a women's retreat and was encouraged by what she shared with me. She has written so many books! I wished I could be like her and share God through writing. Janet believed I could—even when I didn't believe it. Now she calls me "Tami-June." It always makes me smile and reminds me that Janet is dreaming dreams for me. She believes that God will use me, and that brings me courage to try.

To really dream dreams for a friend is more than just believing that God will do something. It requires more than just imagining what is possible. First, it means supporting your friend as she pursues those dreams. It means encouraging her and giving her the time to do what needs to be done to make it happen. I appreciate so much the time my friends are giving me right now to finish this manuscript. They're allowing me time to work instead of getting together with them. Tanya is supporting me by taking care of the boys for a while so that I can have time alone to work and think—time when I don't have to be responsible for anything or anyone else. Sometimes we will be able to support our friends by helping in tangible ways—like Tanya is by watching my boys. By doing things to help the dream come true, you're showing that you believe it will happen. You're showing that you care.

Praying for the dream and for your friend is essential. Sue constantly prays for my writing projects and for my speaking appointments. She prays for all the things that are necessary for the dream to happen, as well as praying about the obstacles that pop up along the way.

Accountability is essential, too, making your friend accountable to doing what it takes. Reminding her that the dream is possible.

Then, when God makes the dream come true, rejoice with your friend. Don't become jealous or intimidated. I know my friends rejoice with me. Cecelia shares my books with everyone. Tanya just saw a review/advertisement for one and saved it to give to me. And Sue's face says it all when I tell her about something new God has done for me in these areas. (And we know it's *all* Him, not me!)

Alan McGinnis, author of *The Friendship Factor*, talks about how to deepen friendships. He tells us that we need to talk about our affection. We shouldn't be afraid to tell someone how much we think of her and how much we value her friendship. That's our next key for a friendship that sharpens one another—letting your friend know how much you care about her, saying, "I love you."

Some people find it easy to put their feelings into words. They can easily tell others that they love them. But for many of us, it doesn't come naturally. We feel awkward or a little corny. But telling someone that you love her will strengthen your friendship. It bonds you together. How do you feel about your friends? Let them know. (And family! Your family needs to hear you tell them of your love for them, as well.) It might be difficult at first. If you can't say the words, find a card that says it all. That is a step. Or say it over the phone; it might be easier than doing it face to face. Tell your friends that you love them. That you respect them and admire them. Share with them what you see as their strengths.

What if your friend doesn't respond? What if she can't say the words?

Give her time. And keep telling her that you care. We have all come from different backgrounds and through different struggles. Some may never have heard words of affection in their families. It is hard for them to put their own feelings into words.

But God can change us no matter what we've experienced. And He can give us the courage and ability to tell people how we feel about them.

Sharing words of affection will enable your friendship to experience the next key—security. Security is knowing that the friendship will be there no matter what. Knowing that whether one of you moves or hurts the other or feels worthless as a person—nothing will destroy your friendship. You feel secure in the friendship.

In previous chapters we've talked about making a commitment to a friend and feeling secure in a friendship. This sense of security is a key to being a stronger person. It enables you to be yourself and to always know that someone will be in your court.

Each of these keys works together. Being transparent, loving each other unconditionally, and sharing words of affection all work to build that feeling of security between two people. As you come to know each other so well, your commitment to friendship is cemented. Such a commitment doesn't have to be spoken. But it will be strong, and so will you.

Our seventh key to a friendship that sharpens you like iron is pointing your friend to God. When you each have a friendship with God, a friendship that is intimate and real, it will deeply affect your friendship with each other and strengthen it as nothing else can. God's love binds us together. The Bible promises, "A threefold cord is not quickly broken" (Ecclesiastes 4:12).

I love to talk about God with my friends and to hear what God is doing in their lives and to share what God is doing in mine. God is so real, so intimately and personally involved in our lives it's exciting to see how He is showering us with His love. To see how He is carrying us through difficult times. As friends, we point each other to God by sharing how we are experiencing God every day.

We can also point each other to God when we're struggling

by asking gentle questions: "Are you praying about this?" "What do you think God wants you to do?" "How are you seeing God working in your life right now?"

When we're in the midst of those dark moments, when we feel that we can't pray, when we don't know where God is and He just doesn't feel very close, we need our friends to point us to Him by praying for us and with us. We need to listen to them pray for us and let them remind us of God's faithfulness through Scripture promises and Bible stories. We need to listen to them as they remind us of how God has worked in our lives in the past.

Pointing a friend to God, reminding her of how much God loves her, helping her to see how God is working in her life, sharing how He's working in yours—these are some of the most important things we can do as Christian women. We talk with our friends about so many things—our families, our work, church activities, the weather, the news. We plan programs together. We pray for others together. We worship together and work on committees together. Through e-mail, we share inspiring stories with each other. We share recipes and books and sometimes clothes. But we need to be sharing God with each other. Talking about Him together makes Him real in our lives; it gives us hope and courage.

Are you and your friends talking about God? Do you know how God has shown your friend His love today? Or what she feels He's calling her to do?

Crystal was feeling worthless. She didn't feel worthy to be part of a church. She wasn't sure that God would even accept her. There was so much in her past that she wished had been different. She was sure that if people knew these things about her, they wouldn't like her. Yet she longed for God. He didn't feel close. She had reached a dark place in her life, and she needed hope.

Trish came to visit Crystal. Trish and Crystal had been friends for a while. They attended the same church and were part of the same small group. They talked about a lot of things—church, people, their families, and jobs. Did Crystal dare to ask Trish the questions on her heart? Could she reveal her ugly past? Would Trish still visit her? Would she think less of her? Crystal blurted out her feelings before she could even think. Trish's eyes filled with compassion, not condemnation. Trish opened her Bible and shared stories of other women with flawed pasts. She showed how Jesus had reached out to them, how He had loved them and forgiven them and given them a new start.

That visit changed Crystal. She knew that God would accept her and love her despite her past. Trish had pointed her to a real, personal God who loved and forgave freely. Crystal found hope and courage to continue. That's what God does. He gives us freedom from our past and from our struggles. He gives us courage and hope for today and for tomorrow. Sometimes we can't see Him; life becomes too tough. That's when we most need friends who can point us to Him.

Of course, we can gain courage and strength in looking to God in the "easy" times as well as when we are struggling with doubts and fears. And our friendships will grow stronger and closer as we look to Him together. Trish and Crystal shared a deepening of their friendship that day on the couch in Trish's living room. Talking about God and their fears and struggles became easier, and they became stronger.

The Bible tells us of many friends. Probably none were as close as Jonathan and David. These two men definitely sharpened one another. Their friendship brought each of them strength. Their friendship had all seven of the keys we have looked at in this chapter. They shared a transparency of hearts that is often unseen in the friendships of men. They loved each other unconditionally. They dreamed dreams for each other. Jonathan dreamed of the day David would be king—despite the fact that he himself was the heir to the throne. He knew that God had called David, and he often reminded David that David would one day be king.

They held each other accountable and talked openly of their affection—even making a covenant of lasting friendship. They were secure in each other's friendship. Even though Jonathan's father was intent on killing David, David knew that he could rely on Jonathan. He knew that Jonathan would always be a faithful friend—even if it meant risking his life and his father's anger.

One of the verses I like best in the story of David and Jonathan is in 1 Samuel 23. It shows how they pointed each other to God. David was hiding from Saul in the wilderness of Ziph. Jonathan went to David. Verse 16 says, "Then Jonathan, Saul's son, arose and went to David in the woods and strengthened his hand in God." David had a relationship with God; he was holding onto God's hand. Jonathan came to strengthen that bond between David and God. He wanted to encourage him in his walk. He told David not to be afraid, that he would someday be the king. He assured his friend that Saul couldn't do anything to him because God was in control.

As we put into practice these seven keys to building strong friendships, we will strengthen our friend's hand in God. We'll also strengthen her hand in ours. As we become transparent, love unconditionally, hold each other accountable in the areas that are important to us, dream dreams and help our friends reach for those dreams, talk about our affection for one another, feel secure in our friendship, and point each other to God, we will sharpen one another. We will grow to be the women God intended us to be—confident, secure, grounded in Him, and growing together in Him.

CHAPTER 9

Mentor Friends

Who would believe her? Where could she turn? Would anyone understand that an angel had spoken to her? Would they believe in the miracle of the child growing in her womb? Mary knew what to do. She remembered what the angel had said, "Elizabeth your relative has also conceived a son in her old age." She would go to Elizabeth.

Mary stayed with Elizabeth for three months (see Luke 1). The Bible doesn't tell us what the two women talked about or did for those three months, but we can imagine. They talked about the miracles surrounding their pregnancies. They talked about what it would mean to parent such a gift from God—the Messiah and the one who would prepare the people for the Messiah. What awesome jobs!

Mary was young; she needed and desired the wisdom of an older woman. A woman who loved the Lord and who loved her husband, because Mary would not only become a mother but a wife. Elizabeth could teach her and share with her all she had learned in her own life. Elizabeth knew what it was to have people talking about her, whispering behind her back. They had talked about her when she was barren, wondering why God was cursing her. Now they were talking about her being pregnant and so old! She knew the gossip—how it hurt and what Mary faced.

I doubt that Elizabeth ever sat down and said, "OK, Mary, today we're going to learn about how to deal with gossip." I doubt that she ever began the morning by saying, "Your lesson for today, Mary, will be how to love and respect your husband and keep a good home." Yet I'm sure Elizabeth taught Mary these things while they were together. As they worked beside each other preparing the evening meal. As Mary watched Elizabeth talk with Zacharias. As Mary shared from her heart her fears and hurts, Elizabeth must have listened lovingly, offering hope and pointing Mary to the God who was so near to each of them.

That's what mentoring is all about. It's a friendship between two people in which one learns from the experience and life of the other. When we think of a mentor, we usually think of someone who is older and who is able to share his or her wisdom, gleaned from years of experience. We're all older than someone. Even if you're in your twenties, you're older than a teenager. That's a great time to mentor a young person in the area of dating and relationships. But a mentor doesn't necessarily have to be someone older. To mentor someone, you need to be more experienced in an area of life. You have to have knowledge, experience, and a willingness to share your life with someone who wants to learn.

Paul was a mentor to Timothy. Not only did Paul write two letters of advice to Timothy that are recorded in the Bible, but he took Timothy along with him on trips. He taught him as they traveled and ministered together. I'm sure the time they spent together was invaluable to Timothy. He learned much of what it meant to be a godly man. Remember that in his own home, his father was a Greek; it had been his mother and grandmother who taught him about God. Paul said that Timothy was like his own son. In the time they shared together, they developed a bond that went beyond friendship—a love as deep as that between a father and son.

In his letter to Titus, Paul teaches the church the importance of the role of mentoring. Even the women of the church were to mentor. "Bid the older women similarly to be reverent and devout in their deportment, as becomes those engaged in sacred service, not slanderers or slaves to drink. They are to give good counsel and be teachers of what is right and noble, so that they will wisely train the young women to be sane and soberminded—temperate, disciplined—and to love their husbands and their children; to be self-controlled, chaste, homemakers, good-natured (kindhearted), adapting and subordinating themselves to their husbands, that the word of God may not be exposed to reproach—blasphemed or discredited" (Titus 2:3-5, The Amplified Bible). The Greek word translated *train* means "to make sane or sober of mind, to moderate, to discipline."

How could these older women train the younger ones? By first living the life themselves. That's why Paul begins by giving advice on how they are to live and follows by telling them what they are to teach the younger women. A mentor can teach and guide another person because she has already learned for herself.

Each of us has different areas of our lives where a mentor could be helpful—our careers, our parenting skills, our marriages, and spiritual areas of our lives. Any area in which we would like to learn from someone who has already been there can be an area in which mentoring would be beneficial to us.

A mentor is someone who comes alongside you and offers friendship. She may offer advice, but it's not a class or training seminar. Instead, you learn as you spend time together talking. The one being mentored may ask questions or share struggles in that area of her life. The mentor can then guide and share what she has learned from her own experience.

A mentor is someone who will have time for us, who won't be too busy to get together on a regular basis. Someone who will keep in touch. A mentor needs to be someone we can get along with, someone whom we respect and enjoy. If personalities clash, mentoring is not going to take place no matter how wise the person may be. It works the other way too. For us to mentor someone, she needs to be someone we like, someone who desires the relationship.

A mentor is someone who listens. One man described his mentor, "My [mentor] listens to me, not like an operator obligated to listen, but with eyes looking into my soul and hands holding his chin, like a man praying intently" (Bob Roberts, Jr., "Training With a Championship Coach," *Leadership* [Summer 1996], 58). A mentor listens as we share our concerns and needs. She hears not only our words but our hearts—our fears, our hopes. As she really listens to us, she can offer us hope and encouragement born out of experience—her experience with what we are struggling with, her knowledge of similar fears and hopes.

Janet has been a mentor to me. She was the director of Women's Ministries in our conference and invited me to be part of the ministry. As we worked together, I learned so much. I listened as she prayed; I watched as she ministered to people. She included me as she planned the details of retreats and seminars. I was soaking it all in, learning, growing. I'd have to say that in the area of spiritual growth, I have learned more from Janet than from any other person. She taught me to pray more fervently. She taught me the power of praise and the difference it can make in my life. And she taught me these things by sharing with me what she was learning herself, by sharing what was important to her.

Eventually, she and her husband were called to another conference, and I was asked to be the director of the ministry in her place. It was scary. I was reluctant at first. But Janet had taught me well, by including me in planning, by sharing the details with me, and by telling me the things that she thought were really important.

Even today, although we live at opposite ends of the country, I still value her opinions and thoughts. I still enjoy spending time with her—even if it's just a few minutes on the phone or by e-mail. She made a difference in my life just by sharing herself.

When I surveyed women about their friendships, I asked, "Have you had a mentor friendship? Would you like to?" Most of the women responded that they did not have a mentor but that they would like one. Many wrote that they felt it would be helpful to them, but they didn't know how to develop that kind of relationship.

How do we begin a mentor friendship?

It can begin one of two ways—either with the person who would like to be mentored asking someone to help guide them or with someone who is willing to mentor another person offering to do so.

If you would like to be mentored, look around you. Whom do you know and admire? Whom would you like to become more like? Do you want mentoring in the area of parenting? Do you have small children and wish there were someone to talk to, someone who could give you advice and guidance? Whom do you know who has already raised godly, obedient children—children who have turned out to be the kind of persons you would like your children to become?

Maybe you know a family who spends time together, who has family worship and close relationships with each other. You'd like that for your own family. Such a family would be a good mentor.

Maybe you've just gotten married, and you'd like the wisdom of someone who has been happily married for a number of years. Is there a couple in your church who are still holding hands after years of marriage? They might be just the ones to guide you as you grow in your own marriage. Or do you want to grow in your relationship with God? Ask God to show you someone who presently has a close relationship with Him and who can help you learn how to know Him better. Maybe you'd like a mentor in your career, someone who can help you learn skills that will enable you to do your job better. Someone who knows how to deal with the pressures of balancing work and faith. Look for a Christian woman who is respected in her field. She doesn't necessarily have to be doing the same work you are.

Approach the person to whom God leads you and ask her if you can get together. Invite her to lunch or to your home for dinner. Ask her if she would be willing to mentor you. Let her know specifically what you're wanting to learn from her. For example, if it's parenting skills, tell her that you admire how she is raising her children and that you wonder if she would be willing to spend time with you so that you can learn how to be a better parent.

Make sure she understands what you're asking for. You're asking to spend time together. You'd like someone with whom you can share your struggles and questions. She needs to understand that you need a friend who will love and guide you as you raise your own children (or whatever the area is in which you'd like for her to mentor you). She may feel unworthy. She knows the mistakes she made raising her own children. She might not feel that she can "teach" you anything. But you're not looking for someone who has done it perfectly. Neither are you looking for someone who will sit down and formally teach you. You're looking for a friendship in which you will learn as you spend time together, watching how she handles her own children, listening to her advice when you ask questions. Remember that having a mentor is not a training seminar; it's a relationship.

I've found that many older woman, who have much to offer, don't feel that that they do. They don't feel that they could mentor another person. Each of us knows all too well the mistakes we've made, the things we wish we could change. We don't feel good enough to guide someone else. But God knows that we made mistakes; He knows that we blew it at times. Yet He still spoke through Paul, telling the older women to teach the younger ones. We don't have to be perfect. We've learned from our mistakes; so can others. And knowing that we haven't been perfect will give them courage, because they aren't perfect either. If we blew it at times and everything still turned out OK, then maybe it will be OK even though they blow it at times too. Whether you've done your job perfectly or made a lot of mistakes (and most of us will have made a lot of mistakes), you still have something to offer another person.

But an older woman doesn't have to wait until a younger one asks her to be a mentor. Older women can offer to mentor younger women. As you watch the young women in your church, maybe God is drawing you to one or two. Invite them to your home. Call them. Offer to spend time with them. There may be single moms in your church who are struggling to raise their children alone. There may be women who are new to a relationship with God. They're just beginning to learn what it means to know and trust Christ. Where are they going to learn how to pray and study? Invite them to dinner. If they have children, have something special for the children to do. Spend time talking. Let them know that you would like to help them—that you would like to be a friend and be there to share their struggles and joys, praying with and for them, and helping them with what you've learned.

As you initiate a friendship, the mentoring process will automatically begin. You don't even have to use the word *mentor,* just ask for, or offer, friendship.

Chuck Swindoll reflected on what his mentor had offered him: "I thought about the things he had taught me without directly instructing me, about the courage he had given me without deliberately exhorting me. I wondered how it had happened. I wondered why I had been so privileged" (Chuck Swindoll, "What I Want to Be When I Grow Up," *Leadership* [Summer 1996], 59).

Having a mentor, or being a mentor, is a privilege. It's a gift from God, an opportunity to learn and grow in a friendship that goes beyond any difference in age between the friends to the things that are important in their lives. What matters is sharing a common interest, a common desire, to grow and do our best and to share with someone else what God has done in our lives.

Would you like someone to come alongside you and offer you encouragement and hope? Are you able to offer encouragement and hope to someone else by sharing what God has taught you? Pray and ask God to guide you into a mentor relationship. Then watch as God changes both of your lives!

CHAPTER 10

The Best Friend of All

In order to be the best friend we can be, I believe we need to have a relationship with the One who is the Best Friend of all. As we spend time with Him on a regular basis, we will be a better friend to others by following His example and by loving with His love.

God is the Best Friend. He is always there. He loves us with an everlasting, unconditional love. He knows all about us yet loves us anyway. He never betrays us. He always wants the best for us. He dreams bigger dreams for us than we can ever imagine. He listens to us—bending down and giving us His full attention. He helps us. Guides us. Comforts us. We can laugh with Him—I believe He is a God who definitely loves laughter! And He cries with us. The psalmist says that He even gathers our tears in a bottle (see Psalm 56:8). He heals our hurts. You'll never find a better friend than God. And He is definitely the best mentor we can have.

As we grow in our relationship with Him, we will become more like Him. Then we will be able to love our friends with His love. We will learn to be a friend to others like He is to us.

As we spend time with Him, we will learn to know His voice and to recognize Him when He is speaking to us. Our hearts will be more attuned to the Holy Spirit's leading so that we will know whom to reach out to and what to do and say. Sometimes God will put someone on your heart. He will reveal needs and show you how to meet them. You need to follow through as He guides you, praying and reaching out to those whom He has placed on your heart.

How do we grow in our relationship with Him? How do we learn to know His voice?

In my own life, God has become a very personal, intimate God. I see His hand at work in my life. I see His leading and His love. I can't imagine my life without Him. He makes me smile and fills me with peace. He's continually teaching me, drawing me closer to Him. I've grown in Him as I've learned to spend time with Him every day. That time has become very special and spreads throughout my day.

I've made my time with Him a priority in my life, promising myself and Him that I will spend time with Him every day. My favorite time of day is the early morning while the rest of my family is still sleeping. The house is quiet; the phone isn't ringing; no one needs my attention; and I can relax and enjoy my time without constantly thinking of what needs to be done.

Sometimes I sleep late and miss our time together. For me, it's hard to set aside the time once I've started my day and list of things to do. Yet I constantly remind myself that time with God is the most important thing I have to do. I've learned to put other things aside until after I've taken my time with my Father. If God is really the most important part of my life, my schedule will reflect that. Strange as it may seem, I've found that when I set aside time for God, no matter how busy my day is, I almost always end up being able to do everything I thought I needed to do anyway.

To make my time with Him relaxed, I keep all the tools I'll need in one place. My worship basket is big; it contains journals, pens, highlighters, Bible study books, devotionals, notecards (for when I feel impressed to write someone a quick note while praying for him or her), my Bible, my prayer notebook, and anything else I might be using. Keeping all these in a basket prevents me from having to get up to search for something in the middle of my quiet time. (Once I'm up searching, more than likely I'll get distracted by something that needs to be done.) It also makes my things portable so I can easily carry them wherever I choose to have my devotional time. Sometimes I like to go outside under the trees. In the winter, I curl up on the couch by the fire with a cup of tea or cocoa. So, I can just pick up my basket and go.

One of the most important things I've learned is to make our time together enjoyable, like time between two friends. It's not just a habit, not just another thing I'm supposed to do. It's a time to enjoy, a time to really get to know God. It isn't something to cross off a list of things I'm supposed to accomplish—"twenty minutes of Bible reading, check; half an hour of prayer, check; OK, now I'm done and can head off into my day." That's not what God intended. He longs for us to see Him as real, as intimately involved in our lives. He wants our time together to be something we enjoy and look forward to each day. He longs for us to know Him as closely as we can know anyone. He reveals Himself to us in so many ways, and He wants us to know Him.

First, He's given us His Word. As we read it prayerfully, the Holy Spirit will make it real to us. He will speak to us right where we are. Have you ever read Scripture and been amazed at how it applied directly to your life at that moment? That's God speaking to you, revealing Himself to you. Sometimes it's easier to read other people's interpretation of God's Word. I love to read, especially books of how God has worked in people's lives and what He's taught them. One of my favorite authors is Max Lucado, who writes about Jesus and the Bible stories in a way that makes me think. But, it's important that I read the Bible for myself so God can speak directly to me through His Word. We must not confine ourselves just to hearing how God has spoken and revealed Himself to other people. Reading what other people have written is good for us—but only after we've spent time in the Word ourselves.

Today there are many translations of the Bible. Choose one that is clear to you. Some people think they should read only the King James Version. King James had this translation made so that the Bible would be available in the common language of the people and they could easily understand it. Unfortunately, with the passing of so many years, the King James Version has become more difficult for us to understand because language evolves and words change their meanings. Choose a version that you can understand and that appeals to you. If you don't understand what you're reading or if it's difficult to read, you won't enjoy it and you will tend to neglect reading the Bible. My favorite Bible is the New King James Version. It has the poetry and familiarity of the King James Version without the old-fashioned English words. But I have several translations on my shelf. The Amplified Version is one I love when I'm studying a specific verse. I also enjoy the New International Version and am looking forward to reading The Message or The Clear Word Bible as well. I read an International Children's Bible to my sons—I want them to understand what I'm reading to them.

There are more ways of studying the Bible than there are

versions of the Bible. I don't stick to one way of studying for long. Sometimes I just read through Scripture, stopping when God speaks to me. Other times I cross reference a specific thought or word. I've also read through Scripture looking for what it revealed about God and kept a journal of what I learned. It was exciting.

You can also ask other people what they have found meaningful in their study of the Bible. Try different methods; use what's most meaningful to you. Remember that you don't have to do the same thing every day. Some days you'll want to sit and just read the Psalms. Other days you may want to study a specific passage or Scripture text intensely. Always remember to pray as you read, allowing your heart to be open to the Holy Spirit.

There are also Bible studies you can purchase and use. If you do, make sure that it's a Bible study that makes you get into the Word. The point of Bible study is to study the Bible.

God also gave us prayer. Bible study and prayer are the two most important ingredients in our walk with Him. God speaks to us through His Word; we speak to Him through prayer. And I've found that prayer has helped me to learn more about Him too.

At one point in my life, prayer had become nothing more than a habit; I was repeating the same words and phrases every day. Sometimes I fell asleep praying at night. Or my thoughts wandered, and I'd have to remind myself that I was supposed to be praying. Journaling has helped me tremendously. I write down my prayers as letters to God. Keeping them in a journal gives me a record of my prayers—something to look back on and see how God has answered. My journals are just between God and me. They're honest. I share from my heart what I'm thinking and feeling. God can't do anything with my thoughts and feelings unless I give them to Him. He already knows them; He just waits for me to be open and honest.

For me, however, praying is not limited to journaling. I've learned to talk to God throughout the day, turning my thoughts into prayers and talking to God about anything and everything in my life. God cares about everything that we care about. He wants us to share our lives with Him totally. He wants to be a part of every part of our lives.

Pray aloud. Pray silently. Pray as you drive and as you cook. Pray for the people who are giving you a hard time—for the driver who drives too slow or cuts you off. Let prayer become an ongoing conversation with God throughout your day.

Praise and thanksgiving have become important parts of my prayer time. I begin my time with God by thanking Him for what He's done in my life. Thanksgiving and praise are two different things. Thanksgiving is thanking God for what He's done; praise is recognizing who He is. Both help us to focus on Him and remind us of what He's like.

I keep a thanksgiving journal and write in it to open my time with God. I thank Him for the things He has done for me the day before. There is always something I can be thankful for—friends, a phone call, something He's shown me, my boys, and husband. Being thankful helps me to recognize what God is doing in my life.

I also praise Him for who He is. God wants us to praise Him—not because He longs to hear good things about Himself but because of what praise does for us. Praise reminds us that God is awesome. That He is in control. That He is mighty and able to do anything. When something happens in our life, the habit of praise allows us to know what He's like and that nothing is too big for Him—that His love is so great for us that He won't allow anything to destroy us. Praise takes our focus off ourselves and our problems and puts it on God. Praise brings us hope and courage.

Music is another incredible way of getting to know God. For me, music—singing, listening to music—is a form of worship, a way of drawing nearer to God. Sometimes I'll be playing music while I clean, and a song will come on that speaks so powerfully to me that I have to stop cleaning and sing along. The moment becomes a holy moment—my heart is drawn to God, and I sense His presence near. I think God loves for us to sing to Him, no matter what our voices are like. He sings for us. Zephaniah 3:17 says that God rejoices over us with singing. Can you imagine God singing over you? Can you picture God delighting in you so much that He breaks into a song and sings in heaven of His love for you? The Bible tells us that He does. Playing Christian music throughout our day helps to keep our thoughts focused on Him.

God also speaks to us through nature so that we can know Him better. Romans 1:20 tells us that nature reveals God to us. Getting to know God can include taking a walk. Looking at His creation. Searching to see the lessons He has for us in the outdoors. What is He teaching you about Himself? Mountains remind me of His majesty and faithfulness, that He is unmovable and a refuge for me. Thunderstorms remind me of His power. Learning about how nature all fits together in a cycle reminds me that He is a God of order and reason. As I watch the squirrels run and chase each other all over my backyard, I picture God smiling and delighting in their antics.

Tim and I recently had the opportunity to explore a little of northern Idaho while I spoke at a retreat. As we walked around a beautiful lake surrounded by towering mountains, I was in awe of God. I knew this was His work. I can't even describe what I felt that afternoon. My spirit seemed to drink in the beauty, and it nourished my soul. What a God who created such beauty just for us to enjoy and explore!

God has given us His Word, prayer, music, and nature—all to reveal Himself to us. He also speaks to us through friends, the church, and opportunities to serve Him. He is constantly at work to reveal Himself to us. To draw us closer to Him. To shower us with His love. To be our closest Friend. God longs to be your very best Friend.

When God is your best Friend, you will be able to be the best friend you can be to others. As you know God and grow in Him, He will develop in you the attitudes and characteristics—kindness, patience, love, faithfulness, and wisdom—that will make you a good friend to others. He will give you the burden to pray for and care for others. He will enable you to help others draw near to Him. He will take away jealousy and competitiveness; there is no need to compete when you're secure in who you are, and that security comes from God alone.

As you grow in Him, you will see many ways He blesses your life. One way is through the gift of friendship. He will give you friends who will bring you joy and courage, who will help you grow and who will comfort you when your heart aches—friends who will make life more fun and God more real.

And your friendship with others will be a part of His gift of friendship to them. He will use you to love others for Him.

CHAPTER 11

A Gift From God

It's been a lot of years since Ann and I played paper dolls on my front porch. The two of us were once inseparable; now we're strangers. I don't know if we would recognize each other if we passed on the street today. So many things have changed since those days of doing cartwheels and complaining about brothers, but my need for a friend with whom I can be myself, who will love me no matter what, with whom to do things, has not changed. Friendship is very important to me.

Making friends hasn't always been easy for me. There have been times that I've been afraid to reach out to others. My insecurities were so big I didn't feel that I had anything to offer. Who would want to be *my* friend? But as I grew in my relationship with God, I learned to accept who I was. I learned that others were struggling with their insecurities, too, and sometimes wondered why *I* would want to be *their* friend. Women too often struggle with feeling "not good enough" or feeling that they have nothing to offer another person. Our insecurities prevent us from reaching out and accepting friendship from others. It often prevents us from being who God has made us. Learning to accept ourselves is an important part of being able to be a good friend. And we can accept ourselves completely only when we look at ourselves through the eyes of God's love and see that although we are struggling and failing, God is working in us and has made us who we are.

Hurts are sometimes a problem too. Some women have been so hurt by friends—often the hurts go back as far as childhood and adolescence—that they've built huge walls around their hearts. They're afraid to let others close and risk being hurt again. Or their life is so difficult that they're afraid to let anyone close. Revealing their pain would be too hard. It's hard to penetrate those walls. These walls keep others out and keep us imprisoned in our hurt and pain. It's only with persistent kindness that the walls begin to tumble, and many of us are too busy to be persistent in pursuing a friendship. When someone resists our attempts at friendship, we give up and go on to someone else, leaving behind a hurting person who really needs a friend.

Sometimes the walls have been around my own heart. The hurt of an ended relationship or a betrayal has been so great that I feared letting anyone else near, afraid that I'd be hurt again. There have been times when I've been so hurt by a friend that I've cried for days or weeks—wondering if the hurting would ever go away. It doesn't always go away, but time has a way of lessening the intensity.

Sometimes my zeal to take care of everyone else has kept me so occupied that I haven't stopped long enough to allow others to take care of me. Then, when I'm discouraged and needing somebody to encourage me, I wonder why no one is there.

As I've written this book, I've thought a lot about friends—especially my own friends. Each has touched my life in her own special way. Each has changed me—some in big ways, others in small ways—but each has left her footprints on my life.

Life would definitely be more difficult and lonely without friends. There have been times when I've been lonely. There have been days when I've longed for someone to call me, for someone to invite me to get together with her. Many times I've turned to God and told Him how much I needed a friend to reach out to me. And He has sent just the right person or a phone call or a note or a visit. Yet at other times, He hasn't. There has been only silence. That's when I know I have a choice. I can sit there alone in my pain, or *I* can call someone. *I* can invite someone over or out to lunch. It's my choice. I can choose not to be alone.

My boys and I have talked a lot about friendship, especially these last few months as they've watched me work on these pages. Friendship is something that is important to each of them; they both enjoy time with friends. We pray for God to bless them with good friends and to make them good friends to others. We talk about what makes a good friend. And we've learned about friendships by watching others.

When Joshua was younger and just beginning school, one of the older boys at school watched out for him. He always chose Joshua to be on his team—even if he wasn't the best player because he was so little. He included him in the things the older boys did, making Joshua feel a part of the group. I challenged Joshua that he could be that kind of friend to the little boys in his school—now that he's one of the older boys.

At camp this summer, Joshua made a new friend whom I could tell he really admired. He told me how this young man was different from most of the other children. He didn't get mad; he seemed to like everyone. He was especially patient with the boys the others found difficult to get along with. As Joshua talked about him, I asked Joshua what it was that made this young man such a good friend. We talked about how to be a friend like that.

We've also talked about the ways friends aren't always nice to us. Each of my sons has already experienced hurts and struggles. One of Zachary's friends was jealous of the time he spent with a new boy at school. Zack wanted to be friends with both boys and hoped that they could be friends with each other. But his friend didn't want that. Instead, he wanted Zack to choose between the two. It was an issue we prayed about for a while. At first, it looked as though Zack had no choice but to choose. He chose the new boy. He said that his new friend didn't care if he played with others. We continued to pray about the situation, and by the end of the school year, God had worked it out so that all three were playing together.

It's interesting to hear the boys reflect on my friendships. They see friendships that are an encouragement to me. Recently we were talking in the car about moving and missing our friends. Zack said, "You would really miss your friendship with Miss Sue. It's hard to have friends like that." I asked the boys what it was about Sue's friendship with me that made it so strong. "You can tell each other anything, and you don't judge each other," was Zack's observation. "It's because you pray together. God is a part of your friendship," was Joshua's response. Sue's friendship is the only one where we pray together on a regular basis. From time to time, I pray with other friends, but with no other friend is prayer a consistent part of our relationship. It's amazing how much our children are watching us! How much they're learning from our example without us ever saying a word. Our children are learning how to be friends by watching our friendships.

Friendship is a gift from God, one of His many blessings

for us. Through our friends, God causes us to grow, to laugh, to be hugged and comforted. And He desires to do the same for others through us. He wants us to be willing to reach out to others. To risk being rejected (didn't He?). To risk being vulnerable. He wants us to be His love to other people.

Close friendships are something we all long for. We all long for someone who will love us no matter what. A person in whom we can confide. A friend who will share our struggles and our joys. A friend to have fun with. But close friendships don't come along everyday. Especially if we don't put ourselves in places where we can make friends. To have friends, we have to be willing to be friendly, to reach out, to be open to having people reach out to us. It's hard for someone to be a friend to you if you never smile, never say Hello, never stand still long enough for someone to get to know you.

As we grow in His friendship, the greatest we can know, God desires us to love and encourage others. He longs for us to be the kind of friend to those around us that He is to us. He uses friendship to show His love to us and to draw us even closer to Him.

It's my prayer that, as you grow in the friendships you have, God will strengthen those bonds and you will grow closer to each other and to Him. I pray that your friendship will be a source of courage and strength and fun. I pray that God will make you the friend He desires you to be.

As you finish reading this, if your heart is longing for a friend but you are all alone, I pray that God will open your eyes to someone to whom you can give the gift of friendship. The gift of yourself. That's what friendship is. It's giving yourself to another person. Don't wait for someone to come to you. Reach out. Ask God to give you courage and to show you to whom you can be a friend. Ask Him who you can love for Him.

May your life be blessed by the gift of friendship He gives you!